Václav Havel

and the Velvet Revolution

Václav Havel

and the Velvet Revolution

by
Jeffrey Symynkywicz

A People in Focus Book

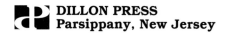
DILLON PRESS
Parsippany, New Jersey

For Elizabeth, with love.

Photo Credits

Front Cover: Filip Horvat/SABA/Time Life Picture Collection.
Back Cover: Wide World.

The Bettmann Archive: 15, 18, 20, 24, 25, 27, 29, 31, 33, 61, 67, 69, 72, 73, 76, 107, 138, 142, 152, 155, 165, 167. Marie T. Dauenheimer: 6.
Wide World Photos: 11, 143, 147, 150, 157, 169.

Library of Congress Cataloging-in-Publication Data

Symynkywicz, Jeffrey.
    Václav Havel and the Velvet Revolution / Jeffrey Symynkywicz—
1st ed.
        p. cm.—(People in focus series)
    Includes bibliographical references and index.
    ISBN 0-87518-607-6   ISBN 0-382-24966-6 pbk
    1. Havel, Václav—Juvenile literature. 2. Presidents—Czech Repub-
lic—Biography—Juvenile literature. 3. Czechoslovakia—Politics and government—1968–1989—Juvenile literature. 4. Czechoslovakia—Politics
and government—1989–1992—Juvenile literature. [1. Havel, Václav. 2.
Presidents—Czech Republic. 3. Czechoslovakia—Politics and government.] I. Title. II. Series: People in focus book.
DB2241.H38S96 1995
943.704'3'092–dc20   94-2384
[B]

A biography of Václav Havel, the dissident Czechoslovak playwright who
spent years fighting for freedom of expression and eventually was elected president of a free and independent Czechoslovak republic.

Published by Dillon Press, an imprint of Silver Burdett Press.
A Simon & Schuster Company
299 Jefferson Road, Parsippany, New Jersey 07054

First edition

Printed in Mexico

10 9 8 7 6 5 4 3 2 1

Contents

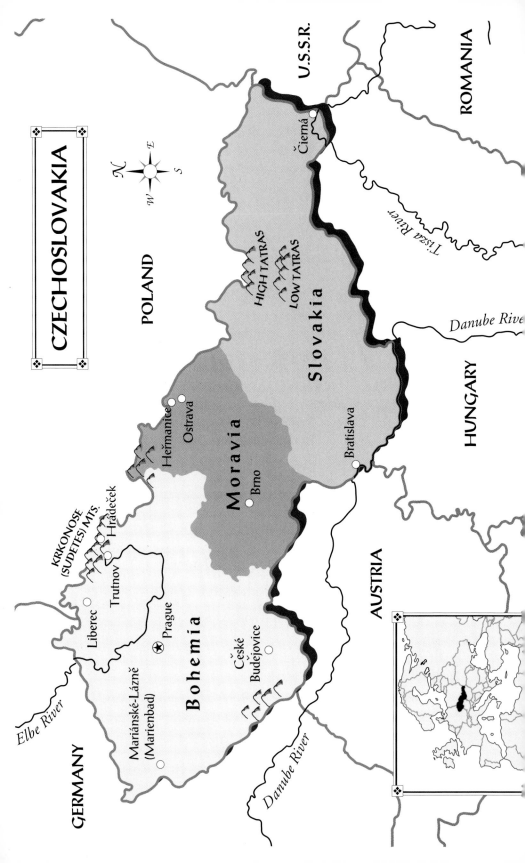

Chapter / One

A Different Kind of Leader

"My people, your government has returned to you!"

With those words, the new president of Czechoslovakia concluded his address. For the past forty years, since 1950, it had been a tradition in that country for the president to make a New Year's Day speech to the nation. This year there was a new man in the presidential chair, a man sworn into office just three days before. His name was Václav Havel.

As he appeared on television, he was dressed in a suit coat and tie, and wore dark-rimmed reading glasses. He was not a large man, certainly—

perhaps 5 feet 6 inches tall. His mustache was neatly trimmed, just above his upper lip, but his reddish brown hair seemed slightly disheveled. Perhaps the new president looked a bit tired as well, and his mood was somber. His serious manner was in contrast to the rest of the country, where the general mood for the past week had been one of joy and festivity. In every city, it seemed, people really were dancing in the streets. In Prague, the capital, there had been fireworks and a huge rock concert in the central square. Of course, people always loved to gather to celebrate on New Year's Eve. But this year the people of Czechoslovakia had an additional reason to celebrate: For the first time in half a century, their country was no longer governed by a one-party dictatorship. This year, at last, they were a free people again.

For many Czechs and Slovaks, Havel's presidency had become a symbol of their new freedom. One could not imagine a clearer break with the past. For the past fifteen years, Havel had become known throughout the country as the most hated foe of the government. The national press portrayed him as a "hooligan," a good-for-nothing, dangerous man, an enemy of the socialist state and of the working people. Indeed, Havel had spent five of the past fifteen years in prison and had been the government's prisoner until May 1989. In just a little more than six months, Havel went from being a prisoner to becoming the president.

And how different he was from those who had held the office before! They had been boring to listen to: always mouthing a lot of statistics to "prove" that life in Czechoslovakia was becoming so much better for everyone, that so much progress was being made. Everyone had known, of course, that nothing really was changing and that many things actually were getting worse all the time. People had just pretended to listen when these men spoke. But now when Havel spoke, people paid attention to his every word. The words flowed with such ease and eloquence that many of his listeners could tell that Havel had spent most of his career not as a politician but as a writer.

"My dear fellow citizens," he began, "for forty years, you have heard from my predecessors on this day the same thing in a number of variations: how our country is flourishing, how many millions of tons of steel we produce, how happy we all are, how we trust our government, and what bright prospects lie ahead of us."

Then he paused, just for an instant, and

added, "I assume you did not propose me for this office so that I, too, should lie to you."[1]

It seemed to many Czechs and Slovaks that they were being told the truth about their country for the first time in decades:

> *Our country is not flourishing. The enormous creative and spiritual potential of our nations is being wasted. Entire branches of industry produce goods which are of no interest to anyone, while we lack the things we need. The state which calls itself a workers' state humiliates and exploits workers. . . . We have polluted our land, rivers, and forests, bequeathed to us by our ancestors; we now have the most contaminated environment in all of Europe. People in our country die sooner than in the majority of European countries.*[2]

Havel would tell his people the truth, even when it was harsh and difficult. Indeed, that was the kind of person Havel had been throughout his adult life: a man who told the truth and lived the truth; a man who refused just to go along with those in power, who insisted on speaking his mind, even when that meant persecution and

Czech President Havel speaks to the media at Prague International Airport after his return from Moscow on June 8, 1990.

even imprisonment. Certainly, this had not meant an easy life for him. Yet, in spite of the challenges he had faced, Havel refused to grow bitter or give in to self-pity. He had always remained a mild-mannered and easygoing man, someone who loved to tell a joke or story and who enjoyed more than anything a night out with friends. He was known as a man who laughed easily, and usually his face was brightened with a smile. He was fifty-three years old now, yet often people remarked on how much younger he looked.

♦ ♦ ♦

Václav Havel was born in Prague on October 5, 1936, the eldest son of a prosperous family. Both his father, after whom he was named, and his grandfather were successful businessmen. Around the turn of the century, his grandfather had built the country's first steel-and-concrete building. His son, Havel's father, continued his work and acquired some of the choicest real estate in the capital. Together they built and managed the Lucerna, one of the city's finest restaurants. They also purchased a hillside outside Prague, on which they built the Barrandov Terraces, a large, fashionable development of homes, shops, and restaurants. Moreover, Václav's uncle Milos Havel was well-known throughout central Europe as the owner of Czechoslovakia's chief movie studio. Havel's mother's family was highly respected as well. Her father had been an editor of one of Prague's leading newspapers; later he had entered government service and had served as ambassador to several European countries.

The family lived most of the year on a large estate in the country. They employed a governess who took care of Václav and his younger brother, Ivan. They also employed a cook and a maid, a gardener who maintained the property, and a chauffeur.

But in spite of the wealth and privilege his family enjoyed, life was not always easy and happy for young Václav. A sensitive and gentle child, he often felt that his family's high social position served as a kind of wall between him and his classmates. Some of the other children at school would make fun of him, both because they were jealous of his status as a gentleman's son. and because he was somewhat overweight. He had difficulty climbing a fence or jumping over a stream or turning a somersault. Whenever he ran in a race, he always finished last. Mockingly, the other boys would call him names. Sometimes they would even slap at his chubby thighs as he walked by their desks in class. While the other children walked home together to farms and small houses in the village, Václav would walk home alone along a cart track through the fields to his family's estate.

Havel spent most of his childhood in a country at war. At the end of the First World War, in 1918, the defeated Austro-Hungarian Empire had been divided into several newly independent nations. One of these, Czechoslovakia, was formed by the union of the "Czech Lands" of Bohemia and Moravia with Slovakia to their east. However, when Havel was only two years old, Czechoslovakia had ceased to be an independent state and had come under the domination of Nazi Germany.

At that time about three million people of German ancestry lived in Czechoslovakia, mostly in the area of the Sudeten Mountains, along the country's northwest boundary with Germany. Adolf Hitler's rise to power during the 1930s increased nationalist feelings among German-speaking people throughout central Europe. In March 1938, Germany took over Austria. At the same time, agents of the Nazi party in Czechoslovakia stirred feelings of discontent among the Germans there. These Sudeten Germans claimed that they were being persecuted by the Czech authorities in Prague and demanded more control over their own affairs. Hitler insisted that he would be forced to take action if such "persecution" of the Germans continued.

Some of the 3,000 refugee families from the Sudeten-German areas of Czechoslovakia, 1938

Tension continued to mount. Many in Western Europe feared that the unstable situation in Czechoslovakia might lead to war with Germany. In September 1938 a meeting was held in Munich, Germany, between Hitler, his ally the Italian dictator Benito Mussolini, British Prime Minister Neville Chamberlain, and French Premier Eduoard Daladier. After long discussion, the four men reached an agreement: In order to avoid war with Hitler, Czechoslovakia must give the Sudetenland to Germany.

Many believed that the agreement at Munich had prevented a new world war. When Chamberlain returned home to London, he declared that the agreement had brought "peace for our time." Hitler had given his word that the Sudetenland was the last territory in Europe he would claim. In Czechoslovakia, however, the feeling was one of anger and betrayal. The Czechoslovakian representative at Munich had not even been allowed into the room as the four great European powers decided the fate of his country. Following the meeting at Munich, one of Czechoslovakia's representatives had complained, "They decided about us, without us."

Hitler had no intention of keeping his word, and started almost immediately implementing his plan to take over the remainder of Czechoslovakia. The Nazis continued to stir up feelings of animosity toward the government in Prague among the Slovaks in the eastern part of the country. In December 1938 the German government announced that it could no longer guarantee Czechoslovakia's independence. The following February, Hitler received the Slovak nationalist leader Vojtech Tuka in Berlin, and the next month Tuka proclaimed the formation of an independent Slovakia. He appealed to his "friends" in Germany to protect his new nation against invasion by the Czechs. On March 15, German troops poured across the border into the Czech regions of Moravia and Bohemia, and Hitler proclaimed that "Czechoslovakia has ceased to exist."

Less than six months later, on September 1, 1939, the German armed forces invaded Poland. Within two days Britain and France took up arms against Hitler. The Second World War had begun.

While the Germans gave their allies in Slovakia some semblance of independence, the remaining Czech lands of Bohemia and Moravia were placed under direct German control. Many Czechs suffered terribly during the long years of the war. All who resisted the Nazi takeover were executed or sent to concentration camps. In May 1942, Reinhard Heydrich, the Nazi "protector" of Bohemia and Moravia, was assassinated by Czech patriots. In reprisal for Heydrich's death, the Nazis executed 1,331 men and women. The most horrible vengeance for Heydrich's death was taken on the small village of Lidice, not far from Prague. There, every male villager above the age of sixteen was taken before a firing squad and shot. All

German troops enter Prague.

the women and children were carted into trucks and sent to concentration camps.

As war raged throughout Europe, living conditions in Czechoslovakia worsened daily. Food and fuel grew increasingly scarce as most of the resources of Slovakia and the Czech lands were used to further the doomed war efforts of Germany.

Prague was spared the heavy bombing that befell many German cities. Nevertheless, air raid drills were common, and, on occasion, enemy airplanes would be spotted in the sky. The sounds of antiaircraft fire and blaring sirens in the dead of night would wake all who tried to sleep. A deep fear enveloped the people of central Europe as they waited for the Allies to advance from the west and from the east and as they worried about where the bombs might fall next.

The Havels' prosperity allowed them to continue to enjoy a relatively comfortable life in spite of the war. There were still trips to the park and the puppet shows, and an occasional visit to the movie theater. Václav began reading at an early age, and his father was determined that his sons would grow up in a house well stocked with the works of the country's greatest writers. Havel's father had many influential friends who often visited the family, both at their estate in the country and at the house they kept in Prague. Sometimes, when they got a little older, Václav and Ivan were allowed to sit in on the discussions that took place around the dinner table. Even though their country was ruled by a ruthless dictatorship, they were able in their own household to breathe a free and open atmosphere where new ideas were always welcomed.

The elder Havel also encouraged his sons to take an interest in history and politics. He told

*Dr. Tomáš G. Masaryk, President of the Czecho-Slovak
nation, signing the Declaration of Independence of the new
nation in Independence Hall, Philadelphia, 1918.*

them about the excitement that had followed the
founding of Czechoslovakia in 1918. Following
the First World War, the Czech leaders Tomáš
Masaryk and Edvard Beneš had gone to the peace
conference in Paris and had convinced the victo-
rious Allies to support the formation of an independent republic of Czechs and Slovaks. The elder
Havel remembered how Masaryk and Beneš had
impressed the whole world with their learning,

their eloquence, and the high hopes they had for their small country. Czechoslovakia had at that time emerged as an example of freedom and decency in central Europe. In time, young Václav, too, came to idolize Masaryk and the other heroes who had been the founders of a free and united Czechoslovakia. Perhaps someday, he thought, the Nazis would finally be defeated and the freedom and decency of which his father had often spoken would emerge again within Czechoslovakia.

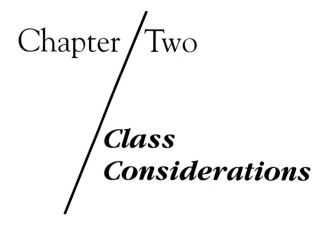

Chapter / Two

Class Considerations

By the start of 1945, Allied armies were closing in on Nazi Germany from all directions. On April 25, Russian and American troops met at Torgau, a city in eastern Germany on the Elbe River, fewer than one hundred miles south of the German capital, Berlin. Adolf Hitler, the once-mighty führer of the German Reich, realized now that his attempt to control the world was doomed. On April 30, he killed himself in his bunker in Berlin, and within two days, the Allied armies were in control of the city. Five days later, on May 7, 1945, the German high command surrendered unconditionally to the Allies.

The people of Prague, too, anxiously awaited the Allied forces. Divisions of the Soviet Red Army, under the command of Marshal Ivan S. Konev, advanced on Prague from the east. Approaching from the west were American troops, under the command of General George Patton. Patton reached the outskirts of the city by May 8; Konev's forces were still at least a day away. However, several months before, in February 1945, the three main Allied leaders—Soviet dictator Josef Stalin, British Prime Minister Winston Churchill, and U.S. President Franklin Roosevelt—had met at Yalta, in the Russian Crimea. There they had made a number of important decisions about the future of the eastern half of Europe. They agreed that Prague would be liberated by whichever army arrived there first. However, within a few months, Stalin changed his mind, and insisted that Soviet troops must be the first to enter. Under orders from his commanding officer, General Dwight D. Eisenhower, General Patton had no choice but to bring the advance of his troops to a halt and await Konev's arrival. Finally, on May 9, the Soviet army entered the Czech capital and "liberated" it at last from the defeated Germans.

The advancing armies, Soviet and American

Marshal Ivan S. Konev, Commander of the Soviet Red Army

General George S. Patton, Commanding General of the U.S. Third Army, kisses a young woman as he thanks her for the cut glass bowl presented to him by the grateful Czech people.

alike, were greeted warmly as they entered the city. Many Czechoslovaks hoped that democracy would be restored as soon as possible. A government of national unity was formed. Edvard Beneš, who had led the Czechoslovak government-in-exile in London during the war, remained as president, and Jan Masaryk, the son of Tomáš, retained his position as foreign minister. The Communist Party, which had led the wartime underground struggle against the Nazis, was rewarded with seven of twenty posts in the new government's cabinet. Beneš pledged that his government would pursue friendly relations with both the Soviet Union and the Western Allies.

During the winter of 1945–1946, Czechoslovakia faced severe food shortages and growing unemployment. Many people, including the Communists, charged that the government of President Beneš was acting too slowly in dealing with these problems. The Communists took advantage of the mounting discontent and gained many seats in the May 1946 elections for parliament (National Assembly). As a result of these elections, Communist leader Klement Gottwald was named prime minister and was given the responsibility of forming a new government. Gottwald named a cabinet made up predominantly of members and supporters of the Communist Party.

Dr. Edvard Beneš

Meanwhile, relations between the Soviet Union and its former allies were deteriorating rapidly. On March 5, 1946, Winston Churchill, speaking at Westminster College in Fulton, Missouri, looked anxiously at the spread of Communism through Eastern Europe and declared, "A shadow has fallen upon the scenes so lately lighted by the Allied victory. From Stettin in the Baltic to Trieste in the Adriatic, an iron curtain has descended across the continent."[1] A new period in history, the Cold War, had begun.

The Communists in Czechoslovakia realized that they would have an extremely difficult time holding onto power within a truly democratic system. They decided, therefore, to take other action to guarantee their rule. In November 1947 Gottwald announced that a "fascist plot" to overthrow the republic had been discovered. All non-Communist members of the cabinet were forced to resign, and Gottwald demanded that President Beneš name a new government made up entirely of Communists. He threatened that Soviet troops might be forced to intervene should Beneš resist his demands. Not wanting his country plunged into civil war, Beneš gave in and named a new government, completely sympathetic to the Communists.

The Communists still were not ready to

destroy the facade of Czechoslovakia as a parliamentary democracy, so Gottwald asked Beneš to remain as president and Jan Masaryk as foreign minister. But on March 10, 1948, Masaryk fell to

Jan Masaryk, Czechoslovakia Foreign Minister, 1948

his death from a window in Prague. To this day, it remains a mystery whether his death was suicide or murder. The Communists then moved rapidly to complete their takeover of Czechoslovakia. On May 9 the parliament adopted a new constitution and renamed the country the Czechoslovak People's Republic. This was more than President Beneš could stand. On June 7 he resigned rather than sign the law authorizing the new constitution. Three months later, he died in his sleep in Prague, and with him passed away the last pretense of democracy in Czechoslovakia. The Communist leader Klement Gottwald became the country's new president.

Now that their control over the country's political life was complete and secure, the Communists moved to remake all other aspects of life in Czechoslovakia as well.

A "personality cult" of Gottwald was established, modeled closely on that of Stalin in the Soviet Union. Banners praising Gottwald and Communism were hung in every town square and on every government building. Portraits of the "great leader" peered down from walls throughout the land. Every day, newspapers would print articles extolling his "great insights" on various questions and celebrating him as "Stalin's best disciple."

Premier Klement Gottwald, June 9, 1948

The government's Ministry of Information and Culture launched a campaign to "purify" Czech and Slovak literature. Seven million books were removed from libraries, bookstores, and private collections and destroyed. The works of most prewar Czech and Slovak writers, including those of the great Czech writers Karel Čapek and Franz Kafka, were banned. Any mention of former presidents Masaryk and Beneſ was forbidden.

Czechoslovakia's minister of education, Zdeněk Nejedly, proudly announced that the Communist Party intended to "change human nature in accordance with our needs." Thousands of teachers were fired from their jobs in grade schools, high schools, and colleges across the country. All were replaced by dedicated Communists. A new course of study that stressed the importance of Marxism-Leninism, the philosophy of Communism, was imposed on all schools across the land. Every student was required to study the Russian language.

The Communist-controlled parliament passed a series of Nationalization Acts, which allowed the state to take over 95 percent of all Czechoslovakia's businesses and industries. Private citizens were allowed to own only very small amounts of property. Within a few years, thousands of factories, shops, farms, and houses were confiscated by the government in its attempts to "liquidate the capitalist class."

Wealthy families like the Havels were no longer privileged members of Czech society.

These victims of the Czech purge have just been sentenced for alleged treason against the state.

Instead, they were stripped of all their property and were persecuted as enemies of the state. The Lucerna, the Barrandov Terraces, and all the other businesses Václav's father owned were taken over by representatives of the new Communist rulers. Forced to move out of its large estate in the country the family was "allowed" to rent a small two-bedroom flat in one of the apartment houses it had until recently owned.

The Havels feared that things might get even worse. The Communist government announced a plan known as Action B, under which all people of "questionable" loyalty were to be moved out of Prague and sent to live in isolated villages near the German border. Soon the government started to round up members of families who had been wealthy before the war, who had served in the pre-war government, or who had otherwise dared to oppose the Communist takeover of Czechoslovakia. Many of these people were loaded onto trucks and led away to the mountains, where they would be held as little more than prisoners in miserable, dirty settlements hidden among the hills. The Havels received their assignment and were told they would be moved within the year to Albrechtice, a small town in the Sudeten Mountains. For months they dreaded the dreary and difficult new life awaiting them. But just before the Havels were to be moved out of Prague, the government lost interest in Action B. The Havels would be allowed to remain in their apartment in the capital.

There, they got by as well as they were able to. Václav's father, once one of the city's leading businessmen, took a job as a clerk in a government office. Václav's mother went to work, too—for the state tourist agency. Her job was to lead tours of the city for visitors from the Soviet Union and other Communist countries. Nearly every day she would leave her job at the tourist agency and stand in line for hours, first at the bakery, then at the milk store, finally at the butcher's or the produce market. It was a hard life, certainly, and they all missed the ease and comfort of earlier days, when the family had enjoyed every possible luxury. But even now they could occasionally splurge on some special treat.

On Sundays, they went to the Lucerna for dinner. The waiters and waitresses there were always pleased when they came, for they still admired the Havel family in spite of what the Communists had told them. The kitchen staff would scurry about and prepare the family's favorite dishes. The Havels would be served enormous portions of dumplings and Prague ham and special sausages from Slovakia, all topped off with apple strudel with lots and lots of whipped cream. The restaurant's new manager, a man who had worked for both Václav's father and his grandfather, would sit with them, and together they would all reminisce about "the old days."

In the "old days," Václav remembered, he had

felt "different" because his family had been so
privileged. He still felt set apart—but now it was
because his family had lost everything they had
once had and because their loyalty was questioned. Nevertheless, Václav did well in school;
he worked hard at his studies and received very
good grades. And he dreamed of becoming a
writer. He would later say that he started to write
as soon as he had learned the alphabet. When he
was only seven or eight, he put together collections of his own stories. By the age of thirteen, he
had already written a book explaining his philosophy of life! As a teenager, Václav spent much of
his time writing poetry, exploring on paper some
of his deepest thoughts and feelings.

In 1951 Václav Havel finished the ninth
grade and prepared to enter high school. Each
high school in Prague specialized in particular
areas of study. Students would apply to schools
whose programs included the subjects in which
they were the most interested and the best prepared. Competition at the best schools was very
stiff, and only a fraction of those who applied were
chosen. Václav loved literature most of all, followed by history and geography. He was fond of
art as well, and music. He looked forward to more
advanced study in all these subjects, and felt sure

that with his high grades he would be accepted at one of Prague's better high schools.

Carefully and thoroughly, he answered all the questions on the schools' application forms. Then he sent them off in the mail and waited. Within a few weeks, all the high schools to which he had applied denied his applications. The reason they gave was always the same: class considerations. The policy of the Communist government was clear. Children of members of the former wealthy classes were forbidden to attend the high schools of their choice. They would have to go to work and learn a trade instead.

Václav started out as an apprentice to a carpenter. On his first day on the job he was told to climb to the top of a roof, where he was shown how to nail shingles. But once on top of the roof, Václav completely lost his sense of balance, and only the quick reflexes of his supervisor stopped him from tumbling to the ground. This happened every time he climbed up the ladder. The carpenter became so intent on making sure that Václav didn't fall that he couldn't get any of his own work done. Obviously, young Havel was not meant to be a carpenter!

His parents were able to find him another job, as an assistant in a scientific laboratory. There he

worked eight hours, six days a week, keeping the
supply cabinet well stocked and organized; cleaning the sinks, floors, and lab tables; and making
sure that all of the equipment was properly maintained. After he had worked at the laboratory for
several months, he was allowed to assist with various experiments, to collect data, and to record the
results. But while he found such work more interesting and rewarding than banging nails and tee-
tering from the roofs of houses, Václav had no
great love for scientific work. Other fields of study
still beckoned to him.

In addition to its regular competitive high
schools, Czechoslovakia had a system of night
schools. These had been established to benefit
older workers who, because of the war, had not
had any opportunity for education beyond the
lower grades. In spite of his youth and his class
background, Havel managed to enroll at one of
these night schools. Six days each week, he would
work his regular eight-hour shift at the laboratory,
and then travel all the way to the other side of
Prague in order to attend four hours of high school
classes. Sometimes his supervisors at the lab
required him to return to the laboratory and work
an additional four-hour shift. Václav followed this
rigorous schedule for more than three years. Even-

tually his hard work paid off, and in 1955, at the age of nineteen, he finally received his high school diploma.

More than anything now, Havel wanted to continue his studies. But one after another, his university applications were turned down. The reason was always the same: his negative "class profile." The authorities who had kept him from attending Prague's better high schools now would do all they could to keep him out of the university. But Havel decided that even if he could not pursue formal studies, he would continue on his own to learn about the art of writing.

While the Communist government held firm control over the publication of literary works throughout the country, there also existed an extensive unofficial literary circle where more daring works were distributed privately from person to person. When he was about twenty, Havel gained enough confidence to pass around some of his own works in this way. He also liked to spend time in the coffee houses of Prague, where the discussions of literature and art would continue late into the night. He attended poetry readings and sometimes went up to the evening's featured authors to inquire about their work and about the latest developments in literature. Soon, Václav

Havel became a familiar figure within Prague's unofficial literary circle.

In time, the political atmosphere in Czechoslovakia improved somewhat. In March 1953, the Soviet dictator Josef Stalin died. Czechoslovakia's president Klement Gottwald, "Stalin's best disciple," attended the funeral in Moscow. On his return to Prague, Gottwald died suddenly as well! Rumors of discontent at Stalin's iron rule began to emerge from within the Soviet Union, and in Czechoslovakia a commission was established to look into the worst excesses of the Gottwald regime.

In line with the somewhat more tolerant attitude developing in Czechoslovakia, the official writers' union tried to encourage "unofficial" writers to take a more active part in the nation's cultural life. Several new literary journals were established, including *Květen*, a magazine aimed at attracting younger writers. In 1956, Havel wrote a letter to the editors of *Květen* defending a group of modernist writers in Prague known as Group 42. To Havel's amazement, the editors published his letter and invited him to a three-day conference for young writers at the Dobříš Writing Home near Prague.

At the conference at Dobříš, Havel spoke in

support of the importance of the work of Group 42. His ideas unleashed a heated discussion about whether literature and art in a Communist society should have any purpose other than to further the building of socialism. Some of the participants at the conference accused Havel of serving "counter-revolutionary" interests and of undermining the state. But others defended Havel and thanked him for initiating the first open discussion the writers' union had had for many years. They invited him to take part in future activities of the writers' union.

But Václav Havel had other matters besides writing to consider. The country required all twenty-one-year-old men who were not in school to serve in the armed forces for two years. Unless some college accepted his application, it looked as though Havel would be drafted into the Czechoslovak Army. Frantically, Havel searched for a school that might accept him. Finally he was granted permission to enroll in a course in economics in the Department of Public Transport at Czech University of Technology in Prague. But Havel had no interest whatsoever in the study of road construction and the lectures on methods of estimating the cost of sand and gravel. After two dull years, he dropped out of the Technical Uni-

versity. He applied once again to the film faculty
of Prague's Academy of Arts. When this application also was rejected, Havel had no other option
but to join the army.

He was assigned to the Fifteenth Motorized
Artillery Division, stationed at Cěské Budějovice,
about a hundred miles south of Prague, not far
from the border with Austria. Havel was part of a
battalion of "sappers," or construction troops,
whose tasks included digging ditches and building
temporary forts and pontoon bridges. In this battalion were many men whom officials considered
possible "troublemakers," including those (like
Havel) of "questionable" class backgrounds. There
were also a number of former prisoners, just
released from jail, as well as other young men who
had recently been expelled from college for
breaking various rules.

Havel hated the mindless regimentation of
life in the army. He wanted to be back in Prague
with his friends, discussing the works of the popular new playwrights. Instead, he was performing
menial, pointless tasks in the Bohemian wilder-
ness. Havel worried whether he would still be
able to think and to express himself at all when
he finally returned to Prague. While Havel was
generally a patient and easygoing person, this

sense that he was wasting his life in the army weighed heavily on him. He did his best to get along with his fellow soldiers. But then one day another private, named Ulver, put out his leg and tripped Havel as he was walking across the barracks. He had meant nothing by it really; it was just the kind of horseplay that soldiers would often engage in to help pass the time. But for the usually mild-mannered Havel, Ulver's joke represented one insult too many.

Before he knew what he was doing, Havel found himself in a blind rage, down on the ground punching Ulver with all his might. He was so angry that the other soldiers had to pull him off. No one could understand what had gotten into him. The years of frustration and indignity, it seemed, had caused him to explode. And poor Private Ulver, author of an innocent practical joke, had to bear the brunt of the explosion.

The next morning Havel apologized to Ulver. From this time, he told himself, he would be careful not to let his anger rob him of his reasonableness and decency. But he knew he had to find some way of expressing his deep, inner creativity. An opportunity came soon.

Not long after this episode, Havel and another soldier, Carl Brynda, received permission to form a theater company for their regiment. The first play the company presented was *September Nights*, a drama about life in the army by Pavel Kohout, a young Czech playwright. Havel took the role of the work's villain, First Lieutenant Škrovánek, a vain, devious hypocrite who plots to become company commander while all the time loathing everything the army stands for.

The soldiers enjoyed the theater company's presentation of *September Nights* very much. However, the next day the regiment's commander called Havel to his office and berated him for portraying the evil Škrovánek so convincingly. Surely, the commander insisted, this was the kind of person that Havel must actually be, beneath his quiet, polite manner.

No, Havel responded to his commander. Škrovánek was an ambitious man who wanted to become company commander. In contrast, Havel's only desire was to complete his two-year stint in the army with as little fuss as possible and go back home to Prague.

The commander then chided Havel for his *lack* of zeal and ambition. He announced that he was going to punish Havel by removing him from the company's artillery corps, membership in which was supposed to be considered a great honor. Havel accepted this "punishment" in stride: It meant he no longer had to drag a bazooka along on drill with the rest of his gear and no longer had to spend time cleaning the gun on his only day off!

The next year, Havel and Brynda received notice of an all-army dramatics competition planned for the resort city of Mariánské-Lázně (Marienbad), in western Bohemia. The two worked hard writing an original play to enter in the competition. The result was *The Life Ahead*, a comedy that gently satirized life in the army. Havel and Brynda delighted in writing the play and in assigning parts to all their friends. The play won first prize in several local competitions, and for a time the Fifteenth Motorized Artillery Division's theater company seemed to have a winner on its hands.

But before the play could be presented at Mariánské-Lázně , it had to be reviewed by a special committee of political officials, who would make sure that it was free of all "antisocialist" ideas. When this committee looked closely at *The Life Ahead*, it came to the conclusion that the work ridiculed the socialist armed forces of the Czechoslovak republic.

Havel, Brynda, and the other members of the

theater group were summoned to Mariánské-Lázně to present their "questionable" work before a special army tribunal. This tribunal also condemned *The Life Ahead* as "antiarmy." In its report, the tribunal accused Havel and Brynda of "neglecting the leading role of the Communist party regimental organization" and other "errors." The playwrights had even shown the poor judgment of portraying a Czechoslovak soldier falling asleep on guard duty, a gross insult to the honor of the socialist defenders of the nation!

The Fifteenth Motorized's theater company was forbidden to present its play at the all-army competition, but Havel and Brynda found a bit of consolation: While the tribunal deliberated, the young men had been able to spend a whole week at the popular Mariánské-Lázně health resort, free of all of their routine duties.

Finally, after two years of service Václav Havel, now twenty-three years old, was discharged from the Czechoslovak army. On the morning he received his official permit to return to Prague, he boarded a train at the station at České Budějovice for the four-hour trip. As he rode through the highlands on the border of Bohemia and Moravia, he wondered what "the life ahead" might hold in store for him. He was a civilian once again, but he had little idea of what line of work he might be allowed to pursue. He had applied for admission to the theater faculty of Prague's Academy of Arts but was rejected. The affair with the tribunal at Mariánské-Lázně, as well as his upper-class background, certainly had not helped his prospects.

Havel hoped, at least, that he would find a reasonably interesting job. But even if he had to find work in one of Prague's many factories, he would save most of his energy for his main interest—writing. From now on, he had decided, he would concentrate on writing for the theater. Working with Brynda and the company's theater group had been the only thing worthwhile about his two years in the army. There was something so exciting, almost magical, in watching one's words come to life onstage. A life in the theater, Havel thought: What a wonderful and rewarding life that would be!

Chapter / Three

From Stagehand to Playwright

There was very good news awaiting Havel when he returned to Prague in 1959. His father told him that an old friend, Jan Werich, who owned the ABC Theater, had agreed to hire Václav as a stagehand. The ABC was one of the last vestiges of the cabarets and vaudeville theaters that had been common throughout Europe before the Second World War. The theater's specialty was comedy: clowns, puppet shows, and, especially, satires that poked fun at various human shortcomings.

From the start, Havel loved his work at the ABC Theater. His busy days were spent preparing for the evening's performance. Every night he would stand backstage and watch as the play unfolded. It made no difference to him whether he had watched the same play the three previous nights. To Havel, each performance was unique and exciting in itself. He marveled at the powerful relationship that existed between the audience and the performers on stage. He was impressed by how a responsive audience could bring out a strong performance from the actors, while a passive audience could have exactly the opposite effect. It was, he said, as though some kind of emotional magnetic field existed between them.[1]

After the evening's performance was finished and the stage had been swept clean and made ready for the next day's work, Havel and Werich would sit together in the empty auditorium and talk about the theater. Havel had so many questions: How was a theater organized? Who chose the plays to be produced? Werich did his best to answer Havel's questions, and Havel felt fortunate, indeed, to have the opportunity to learn from such a master.

Havel remained at the ABC Theater for only a year. In 1960 he took a position as a stagehand and electrician at a new theater that had opened in Prague just two years before, the Theater on the Balustrade. The management of this new theater was young, from Havel's own generation. The Balustrade was interested in presenting more con-temporary, somewhat more daring dramas, rather than the older comedies that were the specialty at the ABC.

With the coming of Nikita Khrushchev and other reformers to power in the Soviet Union, a more open political climate started to develop there and within the satellite countries of Eastern Europe, including Czechoslovakia. The Theater on the Balustrade became Prague's chief center for the presentation of experimental dramatic works. Many of these works were examples of a dramatic form known as the theater of the absurd. Plays written in this style often took place in a world of fantasy and illusion, rather than in the everyday world of time and space. Such plays often utilized a dramatic technique known as surrealism, which attempted to represent the inner workings of the mind or a dreamlike state. Plays from the theater of the absurd often dealt with the relationship of the individual to an illogical, cruel world.

At the Theater on the Balustrade, Havel gave himself over completely to his work. He arrived early in the morning and remained until well after each evening's performance. Soon Havel was called on to fill other positions at the Balustrade.

He was named the theater's secretary, and would arrange for the company to take its plays to other cities in Czechoslovakia. He also served as reader, helping actors rehearse their lines, and worked as assistant to the director. Finally, he was named dramaturge, the person responsible for taking the written script of a play and modifying it, even rewriting it if necessary, so that it could be brought to the stage smoothly and successfully.

Sometimes Havel held several of these jobs at the same time, and it was not unusual for him to work in the theater's office in the morning, run the lights for a play in the evening, and spend several more hours at home rewriting yet another play for an upcoming performance. But Václav Havel did not mind the long hours or the modest salary his work brought. For now, in his mid-twenties, it seemed to him that he had found his life's work.

More than anything, Havel longed to see his own works performed. In 1963 his big break came. The management of the Theater on the Balustrade agreed to present a full-length work written solely by Havel—a satirical comedy, *The Garden Party*.

The main character in *The Garden Party* is Hugo Pludek, an ambitious young man who is good at only two things: playing chess and knowing how to impress his superiors by mouthing the appropriate political clichés. The authorities are impressed by Pludek, who eventually is named director of both the old Office of Liquidation and the newly formed Office of Inauguration. Pludek's job is to liquidate—that is, dissolve—the old office and to initiate the work of the new one. But bureaucrats in the Office of Liquidation, desperate to keep their positions, insist that only their office can do the job of liquidating—a task it cannot perform, because once it would start to close down, the office would cease to be and no office would exist to finish the job! Finally, Pludek comes up with a solution to the problem: He convinces the leadership to name him director of a new government office called the Central Office of Inauguration and Liquidation. Through this governmental monstrosity, Pludek is able to close down the old agency, commence the work of the new one, and secure his position as a rising young star of the bureaucracy!

During this time, too, Havel continued his relationship with Olga Šplíchalová, who was then working nights as an usher at the Theater on the Balustrade. The two had met for the first time ten years before, in 1953, at the Café Slavia, a well-known Prague establishment across the street from the National Theater. Václav had been seventeen at the time; Olga was twenty. She was a strong-willed, outspoken woman from a working-class family, with striking blond hair and a no-non-sense, self-confident manner. Václav was attracted by her unsentimental attitude toward life and her plainspoken common sense. Even back in 1953, he had fallen in love with her almost at once and had wanted to continue seeing her. But no, she had told him, he was just too young . . .

Now he was older. He had spent two years in the army and was emerging as a talented young playwright. When he approached her this time, Olga was more inclined to consider his affections. They started to date again. He was still in love with her; in time, she, too, fell in love. They planned to marry, in spite of the fact that Havel's parents considered her "beneath" his class. But class counted for nothing at all to Václav and Olga now. They shared the same friends, the same love of the theater, the same zest for life, and the same wholehearted individualism that occasional-ly bordered on stubbornness. Olga Šplíchalová and Václav Havel were married on July 9, 1964.

Early in 1965, Havel accepted an invitation to become a member of the editorial board of *Tvář*, the monthly magazine of the young writers' group within the Czechoslovak writers' union. Before long, *Tvář* became one of the most outspoken and popular periodicals in the capital. Because it considered material on the basis of literary merit and not political purity, it published a wide variety of works, Communist and non-Communist alike. Eventually, the Communist Party establishment feared that the articles printed in *Tvář* were moving too far away from the "interests of socialism," and decided to reassert its control over the young writers' magazine. After a long and heated dispute with the party, Havel and the other members of the *Tvář* board voted to close down publication rather than submit to the dictates of the authorities.

In May 1965 the Czechoslovak writers' union planned a large conference to commemorate the twentieth anniversary of the defeat of Nazism and the liberation of the country. Havel attended: It was his first writers' union conference since his speech at Dobříš nearly a decade earlier. So much had happened in those ten years. Yet some things seemed to have remained the same: At this conference, as at Dobříš, Havel issued a scathing attack on the union's bureaucracy and narrow-mindedness. He openly defended by name many of the "dangerous" writers the party still would not allow to be published. Havel also demanded that free and independent journals like *Tvář* be allowed to flourish.

Once again, a heated discussion followed Havel's speech. Many rose to denounce him, while others defended him. The episode illustrated the sharp chasm that had developed within the entire writers' union—indeed within the entire Czechoslovak Communist Party. On one side stood those who wanted to reform Communism and develop a more democratic way of life. On the other side stood the hard-line Stalinists, who believed there could be no compromise, no loosening of the party's iron grip on the nation's cultural life.

The discussion grew so heated and went on for so long that the conference eventually adjourned, unable to transact further business. Single-handedly, it seemed, a young playwright from Prague named Václav Havel had broken up a meeting of the most powerful literary figures in the country! After Havel had spoken, one hard-liner was heard to remark: "This one is going to be a dangerous fellow for us."

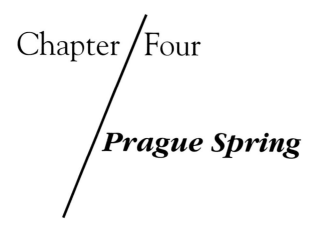

Chapter / Four

Prague Spring

In July 1965 the Theater on the Balustrade presented Havel's second full-length play, *The Memorandum*, a work he had begun writing in 1960.

As the play begins, Josef Gross, managing director of a large business enterprise, is reading aloud a memorandum written in Ptydepe, a new language that the authorities have imposed. The use of Ptydepe, a highly "rational" and "scientific" language, guarantees that one word will never be mistaken for another. In Ptydepe the number of letters in each word is based on the frequency of its usage. (Thus, the most common words will have two or three letters, while the least common word—that for the rare Australian mammal the wombat—has precisely 319 letters.)

All the employees of Gross's enterprise accept the imposition of Ptydepe without complaint, lest they anger the owners and lose their jobs. But Gross, who cannot speak Ptydepe, is unable to make any sense out of the important memorandum with which he has been presented. When he cannot implement its directives, he is branded an incompetent and fired from his high position. He is forced to become a "staff watcher" (that is, a company spy).

But Maria, a sympathetic office typist, helps Gross regain the directorship by translating the memorandum from Ptydepe for him. The memo, it turns out, is actually a severe criticism of Ptydepe—issued by the very same people who had introduced the language in the first place! The owners are now insisting on the use of yet another new language called Chorukor. Chorukor is the exact opposite of Ptydepe: It seeks to make words as much *alike* as possible. For example, Monday is "Ilopagar," Tuesday is "Ilopager," and so on. Gross then becomes the enterprise's most outspoken advocate of Chorukor and regains his old position at the top.

The Memorandum was a great hit in Prague,

and in 1966, Havel was notified that the theater
faculty of the Prague Academy of Arts had accepted his application for admission—*seven years* after
he had last applied. Finally he would have the
chance to go to college. Even though his life was
now a busy one, Havel found time to attend classes at the institute and submit the required papers.
He was granted his degree in 1967.

◆ ◆ ◆

The political scene in Czechoslovakia was
changing rapidly. During the 1960s a group of
reformers led by Alexander Dubček had been
gaining increasing power within the Communist
Party of Slovakia, the poorer, easternmost part of
the country. These reformers demanded radical
changes in the economy as well as increased political openness in the government.

On January 1, 1967, the government's economics ministry unveiled the New Economic
Model, a far-reaching plan to reform and decen-
tralize the Czechoslovak economy. The country's
president, Antonín Novotný, made speeches in
support of the plan but did nothing to implement
it. Instead, he and his supporters clung as tightly
as they could to the old Stalinist ways of doing
things. However, throughout the early months of
1967, Czechoslovakia's economic situation

worsened; a severe housing shortage also developed. Economic conditions were especially bad in Slovakia. Novotný visited Slovakia at this time and in spite of the worsening situation, declared that the "Slovak problem" no longer existed, and that under Communism, Czechs and Slovaks had become one big happy family.

But Dubček and the other reformers within the Slovak branch of the party would not be brushed aside so quickly. At a large gathering of the national Communist Party in September 1967, Dubček charged that Slovakia had borne the brunt of the country's economic disarray. He demanded that the New Economic Model be implemented at once. Then Dubček went even further: He accused Novotný of "acting like a dictator." Novotný, in turn, called Dubček a "bourgeois nationalist"—one of the most insulting things one Communist could call another. The divisions within the highest ranks of the Communist Party of Czechoslovakia were now out in the open.

The atmosphere in the country grew tense. People wondered how far Dubček would dare to go, or when the Stalinist Novotný would finally move to crush all dissent. Students joined in protest against the government. Fearing that the rebels might try to take over Prague, Novotný put

the army on alert. In December the Soviet leader
Leonid Brezhnev came to Prague. After listening
to all sides, he told the Czechoslovak Communists
that their disagreements were an internal matter
and that he would not intervene. Stripped of any
guarantee of support from his large protector to
the east, Novotný sensed that his days in power
were numbered unless he resorted to radical
action. He laid plans for the army to enter Prague
and arrest Dubček and the other reformist leaders.
At the last moment, however, word of his plot
leaked out, and Novotný's scheme was exposed.

At an emergency meeting of the presidium, the
small group of leaders at the very top of the Communist Party, Dubček confronted Novotný with
evidence of his plotting. Novotný staunchly denied
any wrongdoing. Moreover, the hard-liners still
controlled six of ten votes in the presidium and
strongly opposed any attempts to remove Novotný
from office. Finally, a compromise was reached:
Novotný was allowed to remain as president, but
he was forced to surrender leadership of the all-
powerful Communist Party to Alexander Dubček.

Quickly, Dubček moved to appoint reformers
to important party positions throughout the country. Rigid conservatives were removed from the
state security apparatus, and Dubček called for the

Alexander Dubček, 1968

formation of a court system independent of the
Communist Party. On March 22, 1968, Novotný
finally gave in to public demands and resigned
from the presidency. He was replaced by Ludvík
Svoboda, a close ally of Dubček. A few days later,
Novotný and other leading conservatives resigned
from the presidium. It now seemed as though
Dubček and the reformers were completely in control of Czechoslovakia.

At first, Havel was one of many people in Czechoslovakia who looked upon the toppling of Novotný and the elevation of Dubček as merely a "changing of the guard at the top." He did not expect that it would have much effect on the everyday lives of people in Czechoslovakia. In time, however, many Czechs and Slovaks were surprised to see that genuine changes were being made: It seemed as though Dubček was going to be true to his word in attempting to build what he called "socialism with a human face." People began to call the new atmosphere of free expression in Czechoslovakia the "Prague Spring."

As a result of the spirit of freedom that was sweeping his country, Havel was allowed, for the first time in his life, to travel abroad. In May 1968, he accepted an invitation to come to the United States on the occasion of the first American production of *The Memorandum*, at Joseph Papp's Public Theater in New York City. Later in the year *The Memorandum* was awarded the prestigious Obie Award as the outstanding foreign play for the 1967–1968 season.

The United States, and especially New York City, fascinated Havel. He loved the music and art and the free and open ways in which people were able to express their political and social beliefs. In his spare time, he enjoyed walking around the city—from Greenwich Village and the East Village all the way to uptown Manhattan. He felt completely at home in New York's coffee shops and salons, where people discussed the latest developments in writing, art, and politics. Havel spent six weeks in the United States. He then returned to Prague, where the political situation was growing even more exciting—and dangerous.

Brezhnev and the other Soviet leaders were becoming increasingly alarmed by developments in Czechoslovakia. May Day demonstrations in Prague turned into a protest rally against the Soviet Union. In the Soviet press, articles critical of the reforms taking place in Czechoslovakia appeared more and more frequently. Dubček and other Czechoslovak leaders then went to Moscow to explain their position. There, Brezhnev issued a stern warning to get things back under Communist control. On May 8, 1968, Brezhnev called a meeting in Moscow of the leaders of the Warsaw Pact, the military organization of the USSR and its satellites in Eastern Europe. Dubček was not invited.

That same day the Soviet magazine *Literaturnaya Gazeta* published the first of several articles heatedly denouncing "liberalism" in Czech literature. But the reformers within Czechoslovakia felt as though they had gone too far now to return to the old ways. Rather than submit to Soviet criticism, they would respond in kind: Articles critical of the Soviet Union started to appear in the Czechoslovak press, even in official government publications.

On June 26, the provision allowing the censorship of "antisocialist ideas" was removed from Czechoslovakia's national law on the press. The next day, dozens of leading Czechs and Slovaks from all areas of national life signed a manifesto that became known simply as Two Thousand Words. In the document, these influential citizens stated their belief that the tide of reform could not be turned back and that the pace of liberalization ought to be speeded up. They also declared their willingness to defend their country should it be attacked by "foreign forces" (that is, by troops of the Soviet Union and other nations of the Warsaw Pact).

Brezhnev's reaction to Two Thousand Words was almost hysterical. He branded it "counterrevolutionary" and demanded that Dubček condemn it as well. The next day Dubček and the presidium issued a statement disavowing the manifesto. Dubček hoped this would satisfy Brezhnev. But he knew that his people would never of their own free will turn away from the path of reform.

So Dubček also issued a call for "constructive dialogue" between the signers of Two Thousand Words and members of the government.

As part of this program of "constructive dialogue," Havel was invited by the government to a reception for the country's leading writers. It was held at Hradčany Castle, the seat of the government, in the heart of Prague. Havel was still suspicious about the true intentions of the country's reform Communists. Nevertheless, mainly out of curiosity, he decided to go to the reception. At the castle, Havel was amazed by the lavish life-style enjoyed by members of the country's leadership: There was fancy imported food and wine and cognac and champagne. The party went on well into the night.

For the first time, Havel met his country's leaders, including Dubček. Realizing this might be the only opportunity he would have to influence the course of his nation's future, Havel spoke with Dubček at length and advised him to forget about aligning himself with the Soviets. Instead, Havel advised, he should concentrate on using public opinion in Czechoslovakia to isolate the remaining Stalinist elements within their own country. Dubček said little, but listened very closely to everything Havel said. Occasionally, he would interrupt to ask a question. Unlike other Communists Havel had known, Dubček did not resort to slogans and political clichés. Instead, he actually seemed interested in all that Havel and the other writers had to say. Havel came away from the reception finally convinced that Dubček was sincere and truly wanted to establish a more democratic society in Czechoslovakia.

The Soviet Union, however, had different ideas. On July 11 an editorial in *Pravda*, the official newspaper of the Soviet Communist Party, condemned "counterrevolutionary forces" in Czechoslovakia. A few days later, the leaders of all the Warsaw Pact nations (except, of course, Czechoslovakia) met in Warsaw and drafted a letter to Dubček warning him in the clearest possible language that "Czechoslovakia can retain its independence and sovereignty only as a Socialist country, and a member of the Socialist Community."[1] Many believed that the use of armed force to topple Dubček and reinstate the hard-liners in Czechoslovakia might come at any time.

Very concerned about these threats, Dubček entered into talks with Brezhnev. On July 29 a conference began at Čierná, a small town in Slovakia near the Soviet border. Nine members of the Soviet politburo met with President Svoboda,

Alexander Dubček and Leonid Brezhnev

Dubček, and the other ten members of the Czechoslovak presidium. An agreement was worked out: The Soviets would not invade; but in exchange, Dubček must strengthen Communist control over the press, public organizations, and the police and security forces. The publication of articles critical of the USSR was to be stopped. The safety of hard-line Communists within Czechoslovakia was to be guaranteed, and Frantisek Kriegel and Čestmir Císař, two of Dubček allies especially detested by the Soviets, were to be relieved of their government posts.

A few days later, on August 3, the leaders of the Warsaw Pact gathered in the capital of Slovakia and issued the Bratislava Declaration, which pledged each other aid and support. The use of military force to topple Dubček seemed much less likely. But on August 11 the Soviet army started maneuvers along Czechoslovakia's eastern, southeastern, and northern borders. Three days later, the Soviet press resumed attacks on "counterrevolutionaries" in Prague. On August 18, *Pravda* reported that ninety-nine workers at an automobile plant in Prague who had signed a letter asking for Soviet intervention had been demoted. It called this event a grave "anti-Soviet provocation." Then on August 19, Dubček received a long and rambling letter from Brezhnev criticizing the Czechoslovak leadership for not following through on the commitments made at Čierná and Bratislava.

In the early hours of August 21, 1968, the worst fears of the Czechoslovak people were realized. Troops from the Soviet Union, Poland, East Germany, Hungary, and Bulgaria invaded Czechoslovakia at eighteen different points—from the north, northeast, east, and south. Airborne

A Soviet tank moves past the Wenceslas statue in Wenceslas Square after the USSR and Warsaw Pact nations sent troops into Czechoslovakia, August 21, 1968.

Warsaw Pact troops landed in Prague and Bratislava. Dubček and other top government leaders issued a proclamation to the nation, protesting the invasion but urging all citizens to remain calm and ordering state officials to continue performing their duties. Soon, however, Dubček and other Czechoslovak leaders were arrested, put on a plane, and flown to Moscow.

When the invasion came, Václav and Olga

Havel were staying with friends at Liberec, in northern Bohemia. Without hesitation, they joined with the people of Liberec as they tried to resist the invaders.

The radio station at Liberec became one of the outlets of Free Czechoslovak Radio, which continued to broadcast the truth throughout the time of crisis. The Soviets were never able to locate where all the free broadcasts were coming from. When they succeeded in shutting down a station in one area, another would immediately come on the air to take its place. In Liberec, Havel contributed a daily commentary about the events. He even volunteered his services in writing defiant speeches for the reformist leader of the district's Communist Party.

The people of Liberec stubbornly resisted the invaders. They protected the radio station by surrounding it with trucks weighted down with large concrete blocks. They brought a constant flow of food and supplies to those working inside. Even the members of local teenage gangs volunteered to help: The mayor put them to work taking down street signs so that when the invaders came, they wouldn't be able to find their way around town!

However heroically the people of Czechoslovakia held out, their leaders saw no choice but to submit to Soviet pressure. After four days of long and hard negotiations in Moscow, Dubček agreed to Brezhnev's sixteen demands. The situation in Czechoslovakia was to be "normalized"—that is, the country was to return to the Soviet orbit. Censorship of the press was to be reinstituted, freedom of speech was again to be limited, and anyone who dared to resist was to be severely punished. As a final insult, Warsaw Pact troops were to remain in the country to guarantee Czechoslovakia's compliance with the agreement reached in Moscow.

On returning to Prague, Dubček informed the country of the terms of the Moscow agreement. He insisted that accepting Soviet demands was the only possible way to save the country from direct rule by Moscow—and from complete annihilation by more than 500,000 foreign troops.

Gradually the anger most people felt gave way to a sense of resignation, then to feelings of helplessness. Sometimes this helplessness turned to despair: On January 16, 1969, Jan Palach, a young student from Prague, set himself on fire to protest the continued presence of foreign troops. Shock at Palach's death spread throughout the country and around the world.

At other times, the deep anger people felt exploded in rage. On March 28, the Czechoslovak

Portrait of Jan Palach, 1969

ice hockey team beat the Soviets 4–3 in a world championship game in Stockholm, Sweden. In response, large anti-Soviet demonstrations, sometimes violent, swept Prague and other major cities. The Soviet Union filed an official protest and told the Czechoslovak government that if it could not maintain order, the Soviets would do it themselves.

Whatever power they still had after the inva-

A long line of people file past the silver-encrusted casket of Jan Palach, January 24, 1969.

sion soon slipped from the hands of Dubček and the reformers. On April 17, 1969, under pressure from both the Soviets and from hard-liners within his own country, Alexander Dubček resigned as general secretary of the Communist Party. He was replaced by Gustav Husák, who wasted no time in eradicating all vestiges of the Prague Spring.

But while most people seemed resigned to Husák's government and a return to the old ways, others, including Václav Havel, vowed not to give up as easily.

In August 1969, on the first anniversary of

the Warsaw Pact invasion of Czechoslovakia, Havel and nine other members of the Czechoslovak writers' union issued an open letter to the government. This group's "Ten Points" condemned the limits now being placed on freedom and called for a return to reform. That same month, Havel also sent a private letter to Alexander Dubček in which he asked him not to recant his past positions but to hold to them firmly even though everything seemed lost. Havel reminded Dubček that in the long sweep of history, ideas that once seem discredited eventually can become more powerful than ever. Though the freedom and decency of the Prague Spring had been forced underground, Havel wrote, those ideals would remain alive in the hearts of the people of Czechoslovakia and would come to flower again someday.

About a month after the Ten Points were issued, Prague security police came to Havel's apartment. They took him to their station and questioned him for several hours. Finally, he and the other nine signers of the Ten Points were charged with subverting the socialist republic. They would go on trial one year later. There could be no doubt now that the Prague Spring was over.

Chapter /Five

"Dear Dr. Husák . . ."

For a full year, Havel and the other defendants in the Ten Points subversion case waited anxiously for the date of their trial to arrive. Then, just one day before proceedings were to begin, the Czechoslovak Justice Ministry announced that further prosecution of the case had been postponed indefinitely. The defendants were freed—but with a stern warning from the government that their case might be reactivated at any time if they continued to speak out against the Husák government.

A 1970 Communist Party memorandum on the "lessons" of the Prague Spring singled out

Havel as especially "dangerous" to the interests of the Communist state. His name was also included on the official list of banned authors circulated to all schools and libraries in Czechoslovakia. Across the land, copies of his works were removed from library shelves and were destroyed.

Communist Party leader Gustav Husák, October 6, 1969

Husák's crackdown on critics like Havel had its intended effect: People stopped taking any interest whatsoever in political affairs and withdrew into their own private lives. Husák and his advisers believed that if people felt as though their situations were improving economically, they would no longer feel the need for greater political freedom. In order to stifle dissent further, the government took steps to improve the country's living standards. More consumer goods were imported from abroad and sold in state-owned shops. But while Czechs and Slovaks might now be able to enjoy more material comforts than they had before, many nevertheless continued to feel that something important was missing in their lives.

Havel also seemed to retreat within himself during the early years of the Husák "normalization." He and Olga spent almost all of their time at their cottage at Hrádeček, in the Krkonoše Mountains, about seventy miles northeast of Prague. Here he struggled to write, but with little success. Finally, after much labor, Havel completed *The Conspirators*, a play about the rise of Communism in Czechoslovakia. But he was not satisfied with the work at all; the play seemed to him lifeless, its language too unrealistic. He later compared *The Conspirators* to a chicken that had

been left in the oven too long and had complete-
ly dried out.[1] Most literary critics also consider
The Conspirators to be perhaps the weakest of
Havel's works.

Havel realized that if he was ever going to
write well again, he needed to reestablish contacts with other authors and intellectuals. Soon
he and a few of the country's other banned writers
began meeting informally at one another's homes,
and often at Hrádeček. At these gatherings they
would share a meal and discuss a wide range of
subjects. They would also distribute, among
themselves, typed or mimeographed copies of
their latest writings. These self-published
works—known as *samizdat* in Czech and in Russian—were the country's only alternative to the
official literary works turned out by government-
owned publishing companies.

Early in 1974, Havel took a job at a brewery
in the town of Trutnov, about six miles from
Hrádeček. He went to work at the brewery both
because his chief livelihood—being a playwright—had been denied him and because he
sensed a need for more human contact. If he was
ever going to write accurately about the human
situation once again, Havel felt he needed to
expand the circle of his contacts and get out

among people again, back into the "real world" of work and emotions and relationships.

Even though they had heard all about this "political dissident," the workers at the brewery in Trutnov treated Havel as their fellow and equal. But the brewmaster felt that he owed it to the state to keep an eye on a well-known "trouble-maker" like Havel. He installed an eavesdropping device in the cellar of the brewery. In this way he hoped to keep tabs on his most notorious employ-ee and to report to authorities anything he might discover. He also saw the bugging device as a good opportunity to listen in on what the other work-ers were saying about the brewery's management as well!

However, one day one of the other workers accidentally discovered the bug the brewmaster had planted. The angry workers traced the wires from the device all the way back to a listening console in the brewmaster's house. Refusing to return to work, they demanded a full explanation. Authorities of the Communist Party in the area were horrified when they heard about the inci-dent: They were afraid that Havel might write a story about what had happened and publish it abroad. To calm down the local workers, a party official announced that the brewmaster would be fired immediately. A state construction crew soon arrived in Trutnov and ripped out the entire eavesdropping system.

Even as he was working long days stacking heavy barrels in the brewery's warehouse, Havel had already emerged as something of a celebrity outside Czechoslovakia. In 1970 he had received his second Obie Award, this one for his play *The Increased Difficulty of Concentration*. But when he had sought permission to travel to New York to accept the award, his request had been quickly denied.

While all of Havel's works were banned within Czechoslovakia, they were becoming increasingly popular both in the United States and throughout Western Europe. The Czechoslovak government did allow him to receive royalties, or payment, from foreign publication and production of his plays. But government agents also insisted that he spend this precious foreign currency in special state stores so that the government could at least profit a little from his "subversive" works. With a good part of these royalties, Havel eventually bought an elegant Mercedes-Benz automobile with a large, powerful engine—one of the finest cars made—in which he drove to his job at the brewery early each morning!

By early 1975, Havel felt that he had had enough of "private life." He believed that if there was ever going to be any hope for freedom in his country, someone had to challenge the Communist Party directly. In April he took the daring step of addressing an open letter to the most powerful man in the country: Gustav Husák, general secretary of the Communist Party and president of the Czechoslovak Socialist Republic. He also arranged for copies of the letter to be sent to the foreign press and radio stations such as the British Broadcasting Corporation and the Voice of America.

"Dear Dr. Husák," the letter began. Havel told Husák that beneath the calm facade of life in Czechoslovakia, there was a deep fear that crept like the "invisible web" of "a hideous spider" through the whole of society.[2] This fear, though not as harsh and brutal as the terror of the Stalinist period, nevertheless had the same kind of deadening effect on people's spirits.

The present repression, Havel continued, would have long-term negative effects on the nation's well-being. A society based on fear and apathy would eventually become unable to express itself creatively at all. Havel then reminded Husák of how much responsibility he, as both president and party leader, carried for the present spiritual crisis in Czechoslovakia. He wrote:

> *So far, you and your government have cho-*
> *sen the easy way out for yourselves, and the*
> *most dangerous road for society: the path of*
> *inner decay for the sake of outward appear-*
> *ances; of deadening life for the sake of*
> *increasing uniformity; of deepening the spiri-*
> *tual and moral crisis of our society, and*
> *ceaselessly degrading human dignity, for the*
> *puny sake of protecting your own power.*[3]

In closing, Havel called upon Husák and other leaders of the nation to take whatever steps were necessary to guarantee that people once again would be able to speak, write, and think freely. Choosing such a path would not be simple, Havel said, but history and responsibility gave them all no choice.

He signed the letter simply, "Václav Havel, Writer."[4]

Havel had no idea what kind of reaction his letter to Husák might bring. He was prepared to go to prison if he had to. He assembled an "emergency packet"—cigarettes, toothpaste, a toothbrush, soap, books, a T-shirt, paper, and a few other small items—in case he was arrested. For the next several years, Havel would carry this emergency packet wherever he went. He never knew when the police might move against him.

The first reaction to his open letter to Husák was not encouraging. Mrs. Sedláčková, a secretary in the president's office, returned the copy that had been mailed to Husák. In her reply, Mrs. Sedláčková wrote that by making the text available to the foreign press, Havel had already demonstrated his own "hostility" toward his country. He would never know whether Husák actually read the letter or not.

But many others read—or heard—the words that Havel had dared to write. The main points he raised were circulated throughout Czechoslovakia by way of foreign radio broadcasts. Many listened closely as announcers on the overseas stations read the text of the open letter. Some copied it down, word for word. From their notes they made hand-written copies and passed these along to their associates and friends.

Once his open letter to Husák had been sent, Havel looked for other ways to circulate his views more widely. He began to print a series of type-written magazines, *Edice Expedice*, which he would continue to publish on a regular basis. In the columns of *Edice Expedice*, Havel clearly stated his views on important matters in culture and politics. After he and Olga had finished typing each issue, they would carefully tuck the original away in a hidden file and pass along several carbon copies to their closest friends. They, in turn, would make other copies and would pass these along to people with whom they felt safe. Gradually a wider and wider circle of free thinkers within Czechoslovakia looked forward to Havel's most recent essays in the pages of *Edice Expedice*. By the time the *samizdat* copies had been passed along from hand to hand, they were torn and stained; often the print had become smudged and very difficult to read. Still, each word of every issue was studied and cherished—a tiny flicker of truth amid the totalitarian darkness.

In time, Havel felt comfortable writing plays again. He realized that he was no longer writing simply for a particular audience gathered at a particular theater on a certain night. He was now writing for a wider audience, for everyone in Czechoslovakia and around the world who cared about freedom and who would not rest until all people were guaranteed basic human rights.

Soon after writing his letter to Husák, Havel completed a one-act play, *Audience*, the first of three plays to feature a dissident author named

Ferdinand Vaněk. In *Audience*, Vaněk works in a brewery. One day he is approached by his supervisor and asked to become a "self-informer." The supervisor, tired of having to write reports about the dissident, believes that Vaněk—who, after all, is a writer—could do the job much more easily himself!

Audience was quickly followed by the second of the Vaněk plays, *Private View*. In this play, Vaněk visits the home of a young couple who are just "going along" with the government. They try to cover over the emptiness in their lives by surrounding themselves with as many material possessions as possible. They tell Vaněk that he is a fool to waste his time rebelling against society and dreaming of a better world. Instead, they say, he should concentrate on the "real world" of new toasters, washing machines, and fancy furniture.

In that same eventful year, 1975, Havel was approached by Andrej Krob, the director of one of Prague's amateur theater companies. He asked Havel to consider rewriting *The Beggar's Opera*, a play by the eighteenth-century English writer John Gay. The idea appealed to Havel, and within a few months his adaptation of the work was completed and delivered to Krob's company in Prague.

The members of the company rehearsed

The Beggar's Opera for several weeks. Despite the government's ban on the production of Havel's works, the amateur company felt the new play deserved to be performed before an audience. Krob found a private restaurant just outside Prague, the U Čelikovských, in the town of Horní Počernice, whose manager agreed to take a chance and let the company present the play—but only once.

On the night of the performance, the restaurant was crowded with over three hundred of Havel's friends and supporters. Right up until the play began, Havel felt certain that the authorities would step in and stop it. Apparently, however, the local censors did not realize that the play had been written by Havel; they thought that it was merely a performance of a different play with a similar name by the well-known German writer Bertolt Brecht, whose work was not forbidden.

The evening proved to be an exciting, emotional experience for all who took part. Havel was greatly moved by the performance at the U Čelikovských. It had been *seven years* since he had last witnessed a production of one of his own works onstage. (Indeed, it would be eleven more years before he would see another.) He told those present that he had never enjoyed the performance of one of his own works more.

However, when authorities in Prague finally received word that there had been a public performance of a play written by the forbidden dissident Václav Havel, they reacted with anger. The restaurant owner was given a stiff fine and warned that his establishment would be closed down should he show similarly poor judgment in the future. The police brought in for questioning as many members of the audience as they could locate. The Ministry of the Interior announced that, in the future, the government would tighten its controls over local theatrical groups and limit more strictly the works such groups would be allowed to perform.

Around the same time as the affair of *The Beggar's Opera*, the minister of education of Austria sent a personal invitation to Havel to attend the premiere in Vienna of his works *Audience* and *Private View*. However, the Czechoslovak Foreign Ministry issued a stern statement saying that Havel would not be going to Vienna. The work of Václav Havel, the statement said, was not representative of the culture of the Czechoslovak Socialist Republic.

Chapter / Six

Charter 77: Open Dissent–and Arrest

One cold winter night in February 1976, Václav Havel peered out the front window of his house at Hrádeček. A small Czech automobile was making its way up the driveway through the blowing snowfall. Who on earth could that be? Havel thought. Who would be out on a night like this?

It was a friend from Prague. For several hours he and Havel conversed before the fireplace at Hrádeček. They sipped cognac and shared news about their friends. In the course of the conversation, Havel's acquaintance remarked that the next time he was in Prague, Havel should meet with a man named Ivan Jirous. Jirous, the friend said, was emerging as an important force in the cultural life of the country.

Havel knew that Jirous was a painter and poet

and that he also served as manager for several modern music groups. The best known of these was a very popular (but forbidden) rock and roll band called the Plastic People of the Universe. Havel was not generally impressed by Jirous's work, nor that of the rest of the Prague Underground of which Jirous was the acknowledged leader. The Underground was a lose-knit group of modern artists, writers, and musicians who patterned themselves on the hippie movement in Western Europe and the United States. Havel often thought that Jirous and the other members of the Prague Underground tried to be outrageous just to gain attention and not because they stood for anything truly important. Jirous was suspicious of Havel as well. He thought of him as the leader of the "official opposition" whom the government tolerated in order to look more humane to observers from other countries. He also viewed Havel's success abroad as proof that he had sold out to the wealthy establishment in the West.

Havel was hesitant at first to meet with Jirous. But, sensing the urgency in his friend's voice, he agreed to contact Jirous. A month later, the two men met at a small pub not far from Wenceslas Square. Their conversation was somewhat awkward and uncomfortable at first. But as they

talked, Havel and Jirous sensed that they shared
many deeper ideas. They talked for several hours
about the situation in Czechoslovakia and agreed
that the years since the Soviet invasion in 1968
had been dreary and depressing. Jirous then played
a tape recording of some of the music of the Plastic People of the Universe, which Havel had
never heard before. Listening to the tape closely,
Havel heard in their music the anger and sadness
that many people in Czechoslovakia were feeling
through the long, bleak years of "normalization."
As Havel rose to leave, Jirous invited him to a
concert by the Plastic People, to be held two
weeks later just outside of Prague. Havel promised
that he would be there.

The concert never took place. The day before,
police arrested Jirous and all the members of his
band, as well as numerous other members of the
Prague Underground—about twenty persons altogether. Havel was at Hrádeček when he heard
news of the arrests. He knew immediately that
responsibility for leading the group's defense would
fall to him. He also realized that it would not be
easy. Most people accepted the government's
description of Jirous and his followers as nothing
more than "hooligans" and drug addicts. But
Havel also believed that the government had

no genuine political reason for attacking the members of the Prague Underground. They were not enemies of the state; they were being harassed simply because they were "different." Havel said later, "They were simply young people who wanted to live in their own way, to make music they liked, to sing what they wanted to sing, to live in harmony with themselves, and to express themselves in a truthful way."[1]

Through Havel's hard work, seventy of the country's leading cultural figures signed a petition in support of Jirous and his band. Reform Communists not heard from since the days of Alexander Dubček issued statements asking for the defendants' release. The defense of the Plastic People of the Universe awoke other supporters of the Prague Spring from their slumber and set off the first alarm bell of opposition to Gustav Husák's regime.

Czechoslovak officials were taken aback by the outcry. At first, the state pressed forward with its attack on the members of the Underground. A documentary attempting to prove what terrible people the defendants were was shown on national television. When these tough tactics failed to weaken support for Jirous, the government backed off somewhat: Of those originally arrested, charges were dropped against all except Jirous and three others. Their cases were scheduled for trial in September 1976.

As the four defendants were led in handcuffs into the courtroom, they passed twenty or thirty men and women gathered in their defense. Some of the bystanders shouted words of encouragement; others held up clenched fists to show their support. The verdict, of course, was as expected: guilty. But all four men were given very short sentences, just long enough to cover the time they had already spent in custody, plus perhaps an additional month or two. Those who had taken part in the defense of the Plastic People of the Universe knew that they had not labored in vain. Had they not acted, many more members of the Prague Underground might have been prosecuted, and the sentences delivered would have been much stiffer. A victory had been won, yet Havel knew that more work was needed to maintain the network of support they had begun.

At several meetings in December 1976, Havel and eight other human rights activists laid the foundation for an organization to defend human rights in Czechoslovakia. They drafted a statement, clearly setting forth the group's aims. Pavel Kohout, like Havel a playwright, suggested calling the statement Charter 77. This was in honor of the United Nations' Year of Political Prisoners, which was to begin on January 1, 1977.

Charter 77 opened with a list of the basic human rights that all people in the country should be granted: freedom to speak, write, and meet openly; the right to an education; freedom of the press; freedom of religion; the right to establish trade unions; the right to travel abroad and to leave the country if desired.

The Charter continued by pointing out that when the government had signed the international treaty on human rights at Helsinki in 1975, it had committed itself to guaranteeing its citizens all of these rights. In reality, however, the people had not been granted these freedoms. The Charter then listed in detail the ways in which human rights were denied in Czechoslovakia.

Finally, those who signed Charter 77 declared that it was their own "civic responsibility" to defend human rights in their country. They pledged themselves to continue speaking out whenever these rights were denied, and to document abuses and draw public attention to them.

Jiří Hájek, Jan Patočka, and Václav Havel were chosen as spokespersons for the group. Signatures of additional supporters were to be gathered secretly over the Christmas holidays, in the course of the visits and parties that always take place at that time of year. On a specified day between Christmas and New Year's, all the signed petitions were to be brought to Havel's apartment.

Altogether, 242 people signed Charter 77—a much higher number than the organizers of the effort had even dreamed possible. The declaration was dated January 1, 1977, and arrangements were made to smuggle copies to the news media outside Czechoslovakia as soon as possible. Copies addressed to the Federal Assembly and other organs of the national government were to be presented officially on January 7; the night before, each of the 242 signatories was to be mailed an individual copy of the Charter as well.

On the morning of January 6, Havel walked a few blocks through the streets of Prague to the home of his friend and fellow writer Zdeněk Urbánek. There he was soon joined by two other signers of the Charter, Pavel Landovský, a playwright, and Ludvík Vaculík, a novelist. For several hours the men talked and joked, licked stamps, and addressed envelopes. Finally, 242 copies of the declaration were ready to be mailed. Havel, Landovský, and Vaculík then carried several large burlap sacks down the stairs and into the backseat of Landovský's old white Saab.

The three men drove off, but even before they had reached the end of the street, they noticed several police cars following them. Landovský decided to lead the police on a wild chase through the narrow, old streets of Prague. At one point, two police cars trailing each other too closely collided, and Landovský gained ground. But soon several additional police cars were trailing behind at high speed. When Landovský turned onto Pevnostní Street, on the outskirts of the city, he noticed several more police cars blocking the way ahead; he had no choice but to bring his car to a halt. The police ordered Havel, Landovský, and Vaculík out of the vehicle, confiscated the sacks, and brought the three men to the police station for questioning.

Nevertheless, word of Charter 77 got through to the world. The next morning, one of the largest newspapers in West Germany carried its text in full. Soon it would also appear in newspapers in France, Great Britain, and the United States. It was broadcast back into Czechoslovakia by means of international stations like Radio Free Europe. The Husák government could no longer boast at international meetings about its "exemplary" human rights record.

Government reaction was quick. Over the

next few days, state security police brought in as many signatories as they could find. On January 14, Havel was questioned all night by high-ranking police officials. Then, sometime toward morning, he was put into a cell with a young man accused of robbing a grocery store. He would remain there for more than four months. During this time, he was not permitted to contact a lawyer, nor was he allowed visitors of any kind. As of yet, however, he had not been charged with any specific crime. All known leaders of Charter 77 spent weeks at a time in police custody. On March 13 word came that Jan Patočka, one of the three original Charter spokespeople, had died of a heart attack after an especially harsh session of police interrogation.

But in spite of government persecution, the Chartists would not bow to pressure. Steadily their numbers increased. By the spring, their manifesto for human rights carried nearly 400 signatures. By the end of 1977, there would be more than twice as many.

In May, Havel was released from prison to await trial. Five months later, he and three other Charter 77 leaders appeared before the court to answer a charge of subversion against the Czechoslovak Socialist Republic. The proceedings lasted only a single day. Havel, of course, was found guilty and was sentenced to fourteen months in prison. However, the judge announced, the sentences were to be set aside for three years—during which time Havel and the other defendants were to cease all antigovernment activities. If they failed to meet this requirement, they would be forced to serve their sentences.

Havel had no intention of bringing any of his activities to a halt. Opponents of the government now took it for granted that they were under constant police surveillance, and that listening devices had been placed in all their apartments. Whenever they visited with each other, they generally communicated by passing written notes back and forth. If it was absolutely necessary to speak out loud, they made sure that the faucets in the house were turned up as high as they would go, or that the radio or television was blaring just as loudly as possible. In this way they hoped to create enough interference so that the police listening in on their conversations would not be able to make out their words clearly.

The Chartists thought up other creative ways of avoiding the authorities. Over the next two years, Czechoslovak and Polish dissidents held secret meetings in the Krkonoše Mountains, on the border between their two countries. Havel, who generally preferred strolling in the city to hiking outdoors, had to walk to the top of Mount Sněžka five times within a single year. But he admitted that it was worth it: The border guards on the ground never realized that the innocent-looking hikers walking right by their posts were, in reality, the leaders of the human rights group Charter 77, on their way to meet on a mountaintop with their counterparts from the Polish Workers' Defense Committee.

On April 27, 1978, Havel met with seventeen other dissidents and established a new organization, the Committee for the Defense of the Unjustly Prosecuted (usually known by its Czech abbreviation, VONS). The task of VONS was to gather information on human rights abuses and other improper actions by the police and the courts. These reports would then be circulated to government officials, the public, and the foreign press. Within a year of its establishment, VONS filed 155 of these reports.

The Communist government responded to the formation of VONS by stepping up its security activities. In August, Havel was placed under around-the-clock police surveillance. A car occupied by two officers was parked all day at the end of the driveway at Hrádeček. Both sides of the road in front of the house were blocked off, and the police stopped all cars attempting to drive past. Visitors who tried to enter Havel's house had their identification papers checked and were told that they could proceed only at their own risk.

Every time Václav left the house by car, the police vehicle would follow close behind. When he got out of his car to walk around, a police officer with a walkie-talkie would follow just a few steps behind him. When Havel went to the post office to pick up his mail, the police would sometimes snatch the letters out of his hands, read them, and copy down their return addresses. The police even accompanied Havel when he left the house on foot to take the dog for a walk!

On November 6, 1978, Havel returned to Prague to resume his activities as one of the official spokespersons for Charter 77. Here, too, he was followed continually. Wherever he went, a small Czech automobile with three plainclothes police officers inside would follow close behind. If he took public transportation, two of these officers would follow him onto a subway or a bus; the third would trail beside in the car. If Havel stopped to speak to someone while walking on the street, one of the plainclothes officers would photograph them as they spoke. If Havel went into a bar or a restaurant, two of the police would come through the door moments later and sit down at a table next to his. Once the two officers even followed Havel into a public sauna!

Havel assumed that the police followed him wherever he went. One summer he and Olga planned to spend a few days visiting Pavel Kohout and his family at their summer cottage at Săzava. Before leaving Hrádeček, Havel wrote his father in Prague, telling him of his plans. On the way to Săzava, however, Havel missed his turn off the highway and got lost. The police trailing behind quickly passed Havel's car and signaled him to stop. An officer then informed Havel that he was going the wrong way. "Mr. Havel, please, this isn't the right way," the officer said. "We'll show you how to get there, follow us."[2]

The police were not always so accommodating, however. One afternoon when Havel went into a shop in downtown Prague to buy groceries, he came out to find all four of the tires on his car slashed and his windshield smashed. After having the tires changed, Havel drove off—only to be stopped by the police a block down the road and charged with driving with an unsafe windshield! A few days later, someone dumped sugar into his gas tank, gumming up the gas line, fuel pump, and carburetor. Repairs cost Havel the equivalent of several hundred dollars.

Two other police officers spent the entire day at a small table on the landing just beneath Havel's apartment in Prague. Their duty was to check the papers of every person who tried to enter. When foreign reporters attempted to visit him, Havel was pressed into service as an interpreter for the police. It seemed to Havel like an absurd scene out of one of his own plays. Sometimes he would have to translate for his captors the greetings being extended to him from foreign dignitaries: "On behalf of the Foreign Ministry of the Federal Republic of Germany . . ." Then, in turn, he would have to translate the stern warnings of the police to the foreign visitors: "If you know what's good for you, you'll get out of here."

In late December 1978, Olga and Václav left Prague and returned to Hrádeček. As they approached their house in the country, they were amazed to find that an observation post had been built across the road from their property. Apparently the police had tired of sitting in their cold car all day, and wanted a more comfortable post from which to observe Havel! Havel thought that the observation post looked just like a Soviet space capsule, so he named it the Lunochod.

On another occasion that winter, Václav and Olga again returned to Hrádeček after spending several days in Prague. As they entered the house late in the evening, it was ice cold, but when they turned on the furnace, there was still no heat. Likewise, there was no running water. And every drain in the house, it seemed, was somehow clogged. Soon they discovered the reasons for these mishaps. Someone had cut the wires of the boiler's ignition system, had stuffed the water pump with wool, and had poured quick-drying cement down all the drains, and even down the toilet. The authorities were sending Havel a clear message: They were willing to go to any extreme to wear him down and weaken his will.

As time passed, the government increased the pressure on Havel even further. In Hrádeček he was told that he would be allowed to leave the house only to go shopping or to the post office— and only then after having to wait hours for official permission. But while the guards in Prague had been very rude, those at Hrádeček were, if not friendly, at least polite. When they followed Havel into town on foot, they would often make small talk about the weather or the latest sports scores. Many of the townspeople in Hrádeček considered the surveillance of Havel a complete waste of time and money. Some even dared to tell the guards as much; others would laugh at them as they walked by. Some of the local people tried to show their support for Havel by sneaking extra items into his bag or by giving him a discount when he went shopping in their stores.

The stress of constant surveillance and house arrest did take its toll on Havel's health. He would lie awake for hours, until finally drifting off to an uneasy sleep. Then he would awaken with a start when the faces of his captors returned to him in his dreams. He heard their steps behind him even when they were not present. At various times now, he suffered from depression, insomnia, severe headaches, stomach trouble, and high blood pressure. Several times during interrogations he was told that there was a way to bring all his troubles to a quick and painless end: A passport could be made ready for him within twenty-four hours if he were to decide to leave Czechoslovakia.

But Havel refused to submit to the pressure. Instead, he decided that if he was going to be confined, he would make the best possible use of his time and do as much writing as possible.

With Olga's help, he smuggled the latest editions of *Edice Expedice* right past the guards in the

Lunochod. Also while confined, he completed *Protest*, the third of his plays to feature the dissident writer Vaněk. In *Protest*, Vaněk is working for the release of a young man arrested for making "subversive" remarks against the government. The young man is engaged to the daughter of an ambitious television writer named Stanek. Vaněk asks Stanek to help him with the young man's case, at least to sign a petition asking the government to drop the charges. But Stanek is afraid of losing his position and uses all kinds of high-sounding double-talk to avoid taking a public stand.

In October 1978, while still under house arrest at Hrádeček, Havel completed his essay "The Power of the Powerless," which many believe is his most important work. In this essay Havel developed the idea that once individuals begin to oppose an oppressive system—once they begin what he called "living in truth"—then that system is doomed to collapse sooner or later.

Samizdat copies of "The Power of the Powerless" were circulated widely among members of Czechoslovakia's human rights movement. Copies were also smuggled out of the country, to people in the other Soviet satellites in Eastern Europe, as well as to Western Europe and the United States. Members of the Polish trade union

Solidarity later claimed that Havel's essay encouraged them to keep up their struggle for freedom and human rights, even when chances of success seemed most remote.

Havel knew that it was only a matter of time before the government launched a full-scale drive against VONS. The security police were not long in making their move. At five o'clock in the morning on May 29, 1979, armed teams of police moved under the cover of darkness into several neighborhoods of Prague. Fifteen leading figures in VONS, including Václav Havel, were arrested and taken to the Ruzyně Prison in Prague. They were charged with subversion against the Socialist Republic of Czechoslovakia.

Soon after Havel had been taken into custody, an official of the Foreign Ministry came to Ruzyně and informed him that he had been invited to spend a year in New York as a literary adviser to a Broadway theater. Surely, the official said, this was a golden opportunity for him. Think of the comfortable life he could lead in New York! If he wanted to leave the country for a year or more—perhaps forever—the government would not stand in his way.

Havel refused even to discuss the offer. He knew that his responsibility now was to remain in

Czechoslovakia and defend the principles of freedom and justice to which he had dedicated his
adult life. If that meant he had to go to prison,
then so be it.

On October 22, 1979, the trial of the top
VONS leaders began in Prague's city court. In
addition to Václav Havel, the defendants were
Petr Uhl, an engineer; Jiří Dienstbier, a former
newspaper correspondent; Otta Bednářová, a former television announcer; Václav Benda, a math-
ematician; and Dana Němcová, a child psycholo-
gist. No one believed that the six would be given a
fair trial. Their attorneys had been handpicked by
the state. In his opening statement, one of the
"defense" lawyers even congratulated the prosecution on bringing such "notorious" figures to trial.
He then apologized that his client insisted on
entering a plea of not guilty.

All six defendants were found guilty as
charged. Their sentences ranged in length from
two to five years. Uhl was to serve the longest
term; Havel's was six months shorter—four and a
half years in a maximum security prison, on top of
the five months he had already spent in jail awaiting trial. There was one surprise when the sentence was read: Benda, Dienstbier, and Havel were
all to be sent to the same prison camp—Heřman-

Six prominent Czech dissidents convicted of "subversion of the state" and sentenced to a total of nearly 22 years in prison. They are (top row, left to right) Václav Benda, Petr Uhl, and Otta Bendnářová; (bottom row, left to right) Dana Němcová, Jiří Dienstbier, and Václav Havel.

ice, near the city of Ostrava, right on the border with Poland. They would be held more than two hundred miles from their families and friends in Prague.

A worldwide cry of protest followed the sentencing of the VONS defendants. In Paris a French human rights group presented a dramatization of the trial. Similar presentations were also staged in Munich and New York City. Human rights groups throughout Europe and North America launched a petition drive, asking President Husák to pardon the six VONS leaders.

But Husák refused even to consider releasing Havel and his cohorts. He had waited too long for this opportunity to put his most vocal critics behind bars. Perhaps Husák believed that if VONS and Charter 77 were deprived of their leaders, the human rights movement in Czechoslovakia would fall into disarray and confusion. Perhaps he felt that, sometime in the future, the imprisonment of Havel and his co-workers would be seen as a brilliant victory for Communism in Czechoslovakia!

Chapter /Seven

/*Prison*

When Havel arrived at Heřmanice, he was led in handcuffs to the large prison cell that he would share with between twelve and twenty-five other men, depending on how crowded the prison camp was at a particular time. He was allowed to keep a few personal possessions and some clothes. Books, however, were strictly forbidden, although each prisoner was allowed to borrow one book a week from the prison library. Nor was he permitted pens or pencils or any kind of writing paper.

Havel settled into the routine of prison life with as much hope as he could muster. Sometimes, when he thought about the years he had ahead of him at Heřmanice, his heart sank. But Havel also knew that his own attitude would be an important factor in determining how much of a toll the experience of prison would take on him. It would be up to him, Havel decided, to design his own program of "self-care." Since he could not change the fact that he was going to be confined, he must accomplish as much as he could with the time he had.

But very little of Havel's time at Heřmanice could be given over to reflection and study. There was work to do. Havel's first job in prison was as a welder. Even though he had never welded before in his life, his supervisor set his work quota at per-haps twice what it would be in a civilian factory. When Havel failed to meet the quota, his rations at meals were cut and money was deducted from his account at the prison store.

Havel had more success on his next job at the prison: cutting up huge rolls of sheet metal with a large, heavy gas torch. The work was very dull, Havel thought, but at least he was able now to meet his quota nearly every day. But soon Havel was reassigned once again, and was sent to work in the prison laundry. Here, the working conditions were certainly much cleaner, but the laundry was notorious for being staffed largely by informers.

Perhaps the prison authorities had sent him to work there in order to uncover any dissident activities he might be carrying on within the prison. When the informers failed to get any information out of him, Havel was transferred once again and given an especially dirty and monotonous job— stripping the insulation off wires and cables in Heřmanice's scrap metal plant.

The warden at Heřmanice had held his position for a long time, and he viewed the arrival of Havel, Dienstbier, and Benda at his camp as a "reward" for his years of loyal service. He vowed to make life as difficult as he possibly could for the three of them.

On the other hand, most of the other prisoners treated the three dissidents with the utmost respect and admiration. They often would go to Benda, Dienstbier, or Havel when they needed advice on financial, legal, and personal matters. If they needed someone honest and fair to mediate disputes over the rules of poker, they would look for one of the three VONS leaders. When news of such practices reached the warden, he became red with anger. He declared that he would not allow a branch of VONS to be set up in *his* prison! On another occasion, when the warden learned that Havel and Benda had been writing letters for an illiterate gypsy, he sent the two of them to solitary confinement for several days.

There were occasional breaks from the dull prison routine. On Christmas Day, some celebrating was allowed. The inmates were given a full day off from work and were allowed to combine their food parcels and to put out a special "spread" to which everyone was invited. There would be all kinds of treats that the prisoners might not see again for an entire year: caviar, cookies, oranges, nuts, chocolates, raisins, even cigars!

Havel looked forward eagerly to special occasions like these. Indeed, as part of his program of "self-care," he learned to savor even the simplest experiences. Seemingly insignificant activities like mending his socks or drinking a cup of tea became sources of hope and inspiration for him and helped him to withstand the harshness of prison life.

The highlight of each week was the time he had on Saturday to write a letter home to Olga in Prague. Each prisoner was allowed to write his closest relative one four-page letter a week. It had to be neatly written and legible, with nothing crossed out or erased. Quotation marks, underlining, and foreign phrases were all banned because they slowed down the work of the prison's censors. Prison guidelines also stated that letters could deal only with personal and family matters. Prisoners were forbidden to write about politics or the law. Nor were they allowed to include humorous remarks in their letters home. After all, the authorities declared, there was not supposed to be anything funny about life in prison.

His letters to Olga were the only means Havel had of expressing his ideas while he was in prison. He realized how important these letters would be, not only to Olga but also to all the people who wanted to know how he was coping with the demands of prison life. He knew that these letters must serve as his only possible report to the world about the state of his soul.[1] All week long—as he worked at various jobs around the prison, during the exercise break in the prison yard, in bed at night in the minutes before sleep came—Havel would plan his next letter. The entire letter had to be written at one sitting on Saturday, amid the noise and distraction in his cell. He was not allowed to keep copies of what he had already written, and he had trouble remembering from one week to the next what subjects he had already discussed.

Getting the letters past the prison censors was always a challenge. Philosophical musings had to be buried within subjects that seemed on the surface to be dealing with "personal" matters. Havel often had to disguise his ideas by using long and awkward sentences and phrases that he hoped his readers (though not the censors) would be able to decipher. Instead of writing "regime," for instance, Havel used an expression like "the socially apparent focus of the non-I."[2]

Amid all the philosophy in Havel's letters there were also numerous requests and instructions addressed to Olga. Olga was now Havel's only reliable source of information about the world beyond prison. "Above all, write me," he would urge her. "I eagerly await all news."[3] It was up to her to let him know how the movement was surviving in the face of government repression; whether any other human rights leaders had been arrested or had left the country; how effectively the movement was making inroads in various fields of Czech and Slovak life. From the first day of his arrest, Olga, with the help of Havel's brother, Ivan, had taken over the job of publishing *Edice Expedice* and seeing that it was distributed as widely as before. Olga Havel understood completely that it was now her responsibility to serve as her husband's lifeline to the human rights movement.

In spite of the severe limitations under which he had to write, Havel was able to present many deep and profound philosophical ideas in his letters. Even while he was still in prison, copies of some of them were being passed around privately throughout Czechoslovakia. Some of Havel's friends were already developing the idea of publishing *Letters to Olga* in book form abroad as soon as possible after his release.

Life in prison took its toll on Havel's health. One morning in the summer of 1981, Havel began suffering from severe intestinal pain. He was carried on a stretcher to the prison infirmary, from where he was put into an ambulance and transferred to the Pankrác prison hospital, near Prague. There he underwent extensive medical testing and was advised that surgery would be scheduled at some point in the future. While at Pankrác, Havel was able to relax somewhat. Conditions there were much less stringent than they had been at Heřmanice. He also enjoyed being back in the vicinity of Prague, his home, and delighted in spending time each day just staring out the hospital windows toward the spires and towers of the Czechoslovak capital.

After he had spent ten days at Pankrác, the authorities decided that Havel's condition had improved enough for him to resume life in prison. But instead of being returned to Heřmanice,

Havel was moved to the prison in Bory, just outside Plzeň, about ninety miles south of Prague. There, he was told, he would serve the remainder of his sentence. Soon after arriving at Plzeň-Bory, Havel underwent surgery to correct his intestinal problems; following an uncomfortable recovery, his health seemed gradually to improve. He was eventually able to return to work and celebrated Christmas 1981 with the other inmates.

The government seemed increasingly confused over how to handle Havel's case. He was now better known outside Czechoslovakia than he had been before his imprisonment; public concern for him showed no signs of declining with the passage of time. The authorities had greeted the news of Havel's illness with alarm; they realized that the worse thing that could have happened would be for Havel to die in prison. Such a development might have created an international scandal, with demands for a full investigation. Havel would almost certainly have emerged a martyr—even more dangerous to the Communists dead than he had been alive.

High government officials agreed that something had to be done to control Havel's influence. Husák himself decided on the course of action. Late in 1982, he was about to leave on a state visit to Vienna and thought he might announce Havel's release from prison as a sort of present to the Austrian president. He sent one of his assistants to Plzeň-Bory to speak with the country's best-known political prisoner. The lieutenant explained Husák's offer: All Havel needed to do to be released was to write a single sentence asking for a pardon from Husák.

But Havel knew that any request he made for pardon, however innocent it appeared, could be used later by the Communists as evidence that he was admitting his guilt. He flatly refused Husák's offer. The assistant returned to Prague disappointed. Husák left for Vienna unable to make any grand display of "humanitarian concern." Havel remained in prison at Plzeň-Bory. "And," Havel wrote later, "the Austrian president probably got a cut-glass vase instead."[4]

Soon, however, Havel's health declined once again. Late one night in January 1983 as Havel lay in bed, he suddenly came down with a high fever. He broke out in a heavy sweat, and his whole body seemed to ache. Then he began to tremble so hard that his bed shook, waking other prisoners. He was carried on a stretcher to the prison infirmary, where he lay for several days as his condition failed to improve. When his fever began to rise again and his condition worsened, the doctors finally agreed that Havel was suffering from more than a routine case of the flu: He was showing all the symptoms of an advanced case of pneumonia.

Still in his pajamas, Havel was bundled in a heavy blanket, handcuffed, put in a wheelchair, and rolled outside. An ambulance was waiting to drive him back to the hospital at Pankrác, where his health gradually improved. He decided to try to write Olga, telling her that he was back in Prague. He had been forbidden from telling any-one about his move, but perhaps his letter could get through the hospital censors, who seemed much less strict than those at Heřmanice and Plzeň-Bory.

From his hospital bed, Havel wrote one more letter to Olga—telling her all about his latest ill-ness and the trip to Pankrác, and reassuring her that he was going to recover. Václav doubted if the letter would get through to her, but he decided to try anyway.

The letter got through; Olga Havel received it the next day. She rushed to Pankrác and demand-ed to see her husband, but the guards refused to let her in. She returned home and immediately tele-phoned Pavel Kohout, who now lived in Vienna. Kohout then contacted a wide circle of artists, human rights activists, and government officials in various countries, asking them to petition for Havel's release. Over the next week, the Czechoslovak government was flooded with telegrams, letters, and telephone calls, all seeking the same thing: the immediate release of Václav Havel from prison.

On the evening of February 7, just as Havel was about to go to bed, several guards, a doctor, and a government official came into his hospital room. The official informed Havel that the remainder of his sentence had been terminated. He was no longer a prisoner of the state. The doctor and one of the guards helped Havel out of bed, got his clothes, and helped him dress. Within fifteen minutes he was put into an ambulance and driven to the Pod Petřínem Hospital in Prague. From there, Havel called Olga and his brother, Ivan, with the amazing news. A few hours later, he was listening as the report of his release was broadcast on the Voice of America.

Havel considered the month he spent at Pod Petřínem one of the most pleasant of his entire life. In prison he had been merely Havel. Here he was *Mister* Havel once again, and hearing himself addressed in that manner gave him a strange feeling. Everyone was extremely courteous to him now; the doctors and nurses treated him like a celebrity. A steady stream of friends came to visit. Bouquets of flowers arrived from well-known actors and producers, writers and artists, and heads of state from around the world.

It was so unlike prison, Havel thought. Now, for a month at least, he could spend his time as he wished, read what he wanted to, and enjoy the company of the people he chose. Looking back later on the weeks at Pod Petřínem, Havel wrote, "Released from the burden of prison but not yet encumbered by the burden of freedom, I lived like a king. . . . The world . . . showed me its kindest face. I had no responsibilities, only rights."[5] But he knew that it could be this way only until he regained his health. As soon as he was released from the hospital, it would be back to the life of a dissident for him. And—who could tell?—perhaps back to prison, sooner or later. For there was still much work to do, and Václav Havel's deep sense of responsibility would not let him rest for long.

Chapter / Eight

Refusing to Keep Silent

If the Communist leaders of Czechoslovakia thought that Václav Havel had learned his lesson from his experience in prison, they were certainly disappointed. From the first days after his release, Havel made it clear that he would never remain silent in the face of the Husák regime's dismal human rights record.

In August 1984, Havel completed his first full-length play in over five years, *Largo Desolato*. Like most of Havel's plays, *Largo Desolato* is a comedy, but it also presents a chilling portrayal of the effects of fear on those who live under a totalitarian regime.

The main character in the play is Dr. Leopold Nettles, a professor at a leading university. Nettles has written what he thinks is a standard psychology textbook. Unfortunately, the work contains certain ideas that displease the authorities. Nettles realizes that a few ill-chosen words have left him open to eventual arrest—if and when the police finally decide to come and get him. Even though he is technically a "free man," he is paralyzed by fear and becomes completely unable to function. The authorities, however, are in no hurry to arrest Nettles. Merely waiting for them to make their move has rendered him harmless. Why, then, should they go to the trouble and expense of putting him in prison?

In January 1985, Havel resumed his former position as one of the official spokespersons of the Charter 77 movement. The government, taking this as a direct challenge to its authority, would show Havel that his boldness had not gone unnoticed. Within a few days of the announcement of his new position, Havel was arrested by the Prague police. He was held in custody for forty-eight hours and then released.

Then in August, Charter 77 issued a statement commemorating the seventeenth anniversary of the 1968 Warsaw Pact invasion, even though all public references to this period in the country's history were banned. Once again the government moved quickly to arrest Havel. For a second time he was detained for two full days. When, the next week, he traveled to Bratislava, the capital of Slovakia, the police there arrested him and held him in jail for yet another forty-eight-hour period.

But in spite of the inconvenience of mounting police harassment, Havel completed another full-length play during 1985. For many years he had been fascinated by the legend of Dr. Faust, a medieval German magician who, it was said, sold his soul to the devil in exchange for worldly power. Over the centuries, many noted literary figures have written versions of the story of Faust; even before his imprisonment, Havel had considered writing his own version of the tale. Ideas for this work, however, developed slowly. But then, suddenly, in October 1985, Havel saw in a flash the precise form his play should take. He immediately started writing it out. In ten days the entire work was completed.

Havel titled his new play *Temptation.* Its main character is Dr. Henry Foustka, a scientist who works at "the Institute." The stated purpose of the Institute is to stamp out all "unscientific" and "irrational" ideas within society. Foustka, however, has been secretly dabbling in black magic; he is encouraged in this exploration of the occult by a mysterious, sinister-looking little man with smelly feet named Fistula. Eventually Fistula convinces Foustka of his (Fistula's) ability to influence future events. He offers to assist the scientist in his attempts to contact the world of the dark spirits.

However, Foustka's mystical practices are soon discovered, and he is confronted by the Director of the Institute, a vain and self-important bureaucrat. Foustka then convinces the Director that he has been exploring the occult only in order to write a major work exposing the horrible inroads it has made into "rational" society. When the Director accepts Foustka's explanation, his position at the Institute once again appears secure.

The final scene of *Temptation* is a grand costume party in the garden of the Institute. Havel must have delighted in presenting his characters—all of them modern scientists—cavorting around dressed as witches, devils, and goblins. At this party, the Director exposes Foustka's double-dealing and announces that the sinister Fistula has been serving as the Institute's chief informer all along.

On October 5, 1986, Václav Havel celebrated his fiftieth birthday. He now seemed to have more energy than ever to dedicate to his cause. He continued to write; foreign journalists came in increasing numbers to interview him in Prague; Hrádeček remained a center for the activities of Charter 77 and VONS. Gradually the political situation in Czechoslovakia was changing.

On August 21, 1988, the twentieth anniversary of the 1968 invasion, thousands of people gathered in Wenceslas Square in Prague in open defiance of a government order. Those who came were solemn and still at first. The gathering felt almost like a church service, or perhaps even a funeral. Most just stood in silence, remembering the sad days twenty years before when foreign troops had crashed across their country's borders, crushing before them the people's hopes for freedom. A few offered prayers; some sang patriotic songs; others lit candles in memory of Jan Palach, the young student who had set himself on fire to protest the invasion. But gradually, sadness gave way to anger. Thoughts about the past gave way to thinking about the present. Remembrances of Dubček gave way to thoughts of Husák. Prayers gave way to slogans—against the government, against the Warsaw Pact, against President Husák personally. And as though in one voice, the crowd began to shout its opposition to their leaders, a government defended by Soviet troops but despised by its own people. This was more than the police were prepared to accept. They moved in and used force to break up the demonstration.

But the protests continued. On September 23, two new dissident organizations, the Independent Peace Association and the Czech Children, a student group, called an open meeting at the foot of the statue of Saint Wenceslas. Citizens were urged to come to the square and discuss their country's current problems. The organizers of the meeting hoped that they might be joined by twenty or thirty other brave souls; in the past, such a showing would have been considered quite successful. But now, on this day, *hundreds* of men and women answered the call of the Peace Association and the Czech Children. When they saw what was happening, the police quickly descended on the square. Scores of people were arrested. The rest were driven away by tear gas.

In October, Havel and more than one hundred other prominent human rights activists issued a manifesto announcing the formation of another new organization, the Movement for Civil Liberties. The group called for a complete reform of the nation's legal system, protection of human rights, and the immediate removal of all Soviet troops from the country. As Havel was leaving the meeting that announced the founding of the new movement, he was surrounded by a team of police officers and hustled into a squad car. He was driven to a prison in the center of Prague and held in solitary confinement for four days.

Havel was still in prison on October 28, 1988, when the day came that marked the seventieth anniversary of the founding of the pre-Communist Czechoslovak Republic. Havel would not be able to join in celebration of the event, but there were now others to take his place: Nearly five thousand people gathered in the square to celebrate the memory of Masaryk and Beneš and their compatriots. Such a massive demonstration of independent thought engendered a massive police response. The demonstrators had barely assembled before they were dispersed by water cannons and tear gas.

"An electric tension has struck the society," Havel told an interviewer. "It is becoming more restless; it is becoming more interested in everything; people are more daring, they are overcoming their fear, as if they were awakening from that long apathy."[1]

But Gustav Husák could not recognize that times truly were changing. He would demonstrate beyond doubt that, in spite of the reforms sweeping the Soviet Union and the other Communist states of Eastern Europe, the old guard was still in charge in Prague. There would be no return to the liberal days of the Prague Spring as long as Gustav Husák ruled Czechoslovakia.

In November 1988, several dissident groups, including Charter 77, planned an international conference to discuss the importance of Czechoslovakia in the history of Europe. Many distinguished foreign visitors had come to Prague for the conference, yet the day before it was to begin, police guards were sent to the homes of thirty-eight of its organizers. All were forbidden to leave their residences until further notice. But the police were unable to find Havel! Fearing that the authorities might try to stop him from addressing the international gathering, he had gone into hiding. The next morning he managed to get to the hotel where the conference was being held. He made his way to the podium at the front, welcomed the assembled guests, and declared the conference open. But he had spoken no more than thirty seconds when his microphone went dead. A group of security officers marched to the front of the hall, surrounded him, and then led him away to a waiting automobile. After he was driven back to his apartment in Prague, Havel joined the thirty-eight other organizers of the conference under house arrest for the remainder of the week.

As New Year's Day 1989 neared, Havel was interviewed by a correspondent from the Voice of America. He discussed the situation in his country at length, expressing his hope that people were finally willing to stand up for things in which they believed. He noted that the twentieth anniversary of the suicide of Jan Palach was approaching, on January 16; he suggested that perhaps the citizens of Czechoslovakia should find some appropriate way to mark such an important date.

Havel was one of twenty-six people who made their way to Wenceslas Square early on the morning of January 15. They had decided to go there simply to lay a wreath, to place flowers at the spot where Palach had set himself on fire. But before they could reach the square, they were met by police who ordered them to turn back.

The next day, eight of them, including Havel, followed eight different routes through Prague to the square. When Havel arrived at the spot where Palach had died, he watched as a friend laid a bouquet of fresh flowers on the pavement. Within seconds, all eight demonstrators were placed under arrest.

But where eight had come to place flowers,

hundreds came the next day, and the next—and
every single day for a week—to protest these
arrests. The police response was rigidly consistent:
clubs, water cannons, tear gas, and more arrests.
When Havel appeared before the Prague civil
court, he was charged with inciting citizens to
hold an illegal assembly. His trial was over within
a matter of hours. Obviously the authorities wanted him out of the way as quickly as possible. The
case against Havel was so flimsy that the presiding
judge remarked on its weakness. Even she had
doubts as to whether placing flowers in a public
square should be a punishable offense. Yet the
judge found Havel guilty as charged and sentenced
him to nine months in jail. Later, Havel said,
"The verdict would have been far more honest
had it merely stated, 'Václav Havel, you are getting on our nerves, and so you will go to prison for
nine months.'"[2] Havel's new prison sentence
unleashed an unprecedented outpouring of protest
from within Czechoslovakia, as well as from
beyond its borders. Thousands of members of the
country's official artistic and scientific communi-
ties signed petitions demanding Havel's release.
Husák could no longer pretend that Havel's supporters were only a ragtag group of dissidents and
malcontents. They now included many of the

leading lights of Czechoslovak society.

On appeal, Havel's prison sentence was reduced to eight months, and he was assigned to a less restrictive prison. And soon the government began to make arrangements to release him on May 15, two weeks before a meeting of the nations that had signed the Helsinki accord on human rights. Czechoslovakia's leaders did not want to face the embarrassment of having their delegates speaking out forcefully in defense of freedom of speech and assembly while their nation's best-known writer remained in prison for the "crime" of laying a wreath! Havel was released from prison after serving half of his eight month sentence.

Havel wasted no time after being freed. He knew that the human rights movement was growing stronger with each passing week. He helped to draw up a petition called A Few Sentences, aimed at uniting as many Czechs and Slovaks as possible in defense of freedom and human rights. The response to A Few Sentences was overwhelming. Tens of thousands of people from all walks of life now willingly signed a petition that a year before all but a handful would have spurned as "too dangerous." As walls began to crumble throughout central and Eastern Europe, the people of Czechoslovakia, too, were seizing the chance to be free.

Chapter / Nine

The Velvet Revolution

The self-confidence of the human rights movement in Czechoslovakia was on the rise. The government of Gustav Husák seemed increasingly
confused by the rapidly changing situation. On
the one hand, Husák wanted to appear supportive
of the Soviet reform leader Mikhail Gorbachev
and his policies of openness (often referred in the
U.S. press by its Russian name, *glasnost*) and
restructuring (*perestroika*). On the other hand,
government hard-liners remained adamantly
opposed to any reforms that might diminish their
powers.

In October 1989, police units moved quickly

to disperse demonstrators as they attempted to gather in the center of Prague to commemorate the seventy-first anniversary of the founding of the Czechoslovak Republic. The force with which the demonstration was broken up was widely viewed as an indication that Husák had no intention of loosening his grip on the country. The night before the anniversary, Havel had been at home with the flu. In spite of his illness, the state security police forced their way into his apartment and carried him out of bed and into a waiting police wagon. He was taken to Prague's central police station and held for forty-eight hours. The police would make sure that he would be unable to join in the demonstrations commemorating the founding of the democratic state.

About a month later, however, the government did give permission to a student organization to hold an open-air meeting in Prague to mark the fiftieth anniversary of the death of Jan Opletal, a Czech-Jewish student killed by the Nazis. The authorities agreed to allow the students to gather at Opletal's grave in a cemetery in Prague's Old Town district, about a mile from Wenceslas Square.

On the morning of November 17, tens of thousands of people packed the old cemetery and neighboring streets. Most of those present could not see or hear the brief ceremony around the young martyr's grave. But they were there not only to remember the Nazi era but also to secure a place for Czechoslovakia in the historical tide that was now sweeping Eastern Europe.

As soon as the ceremony at Opletal's grave was over, some of the demonstrators began chanting slogans against the Communist government. Others began to sing "We Shall Overcome," which had become the anthem of the civil rights movement in the United States. Now the same song, sung in Czech and in Slovak, swelled from the students of Prague as they marched out of the cemetery. And the cry that most often filled the air was "*Svoboda!*" "Freedom!"

The march moved on...beyond the cemetery ...then out of the old district...past the historic Charles Bridge, and along the embankment of the Vltava River...then a turn at the National The-ater...onto Národní Třida(Avenue of the People) ...and finally into Wenceslas Square.

When the students arrived at the square, riot police were waiting for them. The government had also mobilized a special antiterrorist squadron, the Red Berets. Students in the front lines of the march tried to hand bunches of flowers to the police. Others placed lighted candles on the ground, then held up their arms and announced, "We have bare hands. We are not armed."

For just an instant, there was a brief pause, as the two sides faced each other. Then the security police, led by the Red Berets, made their move. One brigade was dispatched to the end of the avenue leading into the square, preventing the escape of any marchers who might try to flee. Truncheons flailing, the Red Berets marched directly into the line of protesters. Row after row of unarmed civilians fell to the ground. As each row fell, the police trampled over them, straight ahead, ready to pummel the next row of victims. Then the police fired tear gas canisters to clear any stragglers from the area. Within minutes, not a single soul remained standing in Wenceslas Square.

There were reports that one student had been killed. Prague's hospitals were filled with dozens—perhaps hundreds—who had been injured.

Early the next day—Saturday, November 18—students at various schools throughout the capital voted to call a strike. That afternoon, the actors' union became the first organization openly to side with the students. A mass meeting of students and actors was held at the Realistic Theater. One speaker after another rose to denounce the "massacre of November 17." Then a decision was reached: There would be a general strike nine days later, on November 27. All the people of the country would be given the chance to stand up against police brutality and in support of human rights.

Havel was at Hrádeček when he first heard the news of the violence in the capital. Immediately, he hurried back to Prague. On the evening of Sunday, November 19, representatives of several dissident groups met at another Prague theater, the Dramatic Club. Those present agreed to form an organization to coordinate opposition to the government. They called their new organization Civic Forum, and chose Václav Havel to serve as their leader. While the Civic Forum was being organized in Prague, a similar group, Public Against Violence, was being formed in Bratislava to lead the people's movement in Slovakia.

Over the weekend, tens of thousands of students had gathered in Wenceslas Square. In spite of the seriousness of the events of the week, the atmosphere was high-spirited and almost festive. Groups of students climbed atop the mounted statue of Saint Wenceslas. Walls along the square were hung with brightly colored banners and murals. Throughout the weekend the crowds grew larger. By Monday it had become obvious that this was more than just another student protest. People of all ages and life-styles jammed the square, and the tens of thousands became *hundreds* of thousands. Their shouts—"Freedom!" "Resign!" "Now is the time!"—shook the centuries-old baroque-style buildings in the heart of the capital.

The next day, Tuesday, the crowds grew even larger. As on the day before, the number of people in the square mounted steadily all day, and reached its peak in the late afternoon, when workers leaving their jobs went straight to the demonstrations. Prague's subway line was jammed—everyone, it seemed, was heading toward Wenceslas Square. On Tuesday afternoon Václav Havel addressed the crowd for the first time. He stood alone on a balcony overlooking the square as hundreds of thousands of his fellow citizens cheered wildly below. He repeated the Civic Forum's main demands and reminded the crowd of the general strike, now less than a week away. A new cry—"Strike! Strike!"—shook the buildings in the square.

Somehow, through Wednesday and Thursday, too, the crowds continued to grow—eventually to at least a half million people. Wenceslas Square

looked like an ocean of people, and it seemed that not even a single inch was unoccupied.

Meanwhile in his office at Hradčany, Prague's ancient castle, President Husák heard the latest reports of the demonstrations. His government was completely unprepared for this turn of events. The crowds were now just too large to be dispersed. Police units—even the antiterrorist squads—would be no match for masses of people like these. And, Husák knew, there would be no assistance from the Warsaw Pact this time. Gorbachev had been very clear about one thing on his last visit to Prague: Moscow would now view relations between the Czechoslovak government and its critics as a strictly internal matter. The Czechs and Slovaks would have to solve their own problems.

Husák considered the options remaining open to him. Perhaps he could send in the army. Armed infantry, even tanks, could drive right into the heart of Prague to clear the square. But the loss of life would be terrible. As blood flowed in the streets and the protesters screamed in anguish, the entire scene would be televised around the world. Husák would be considered an international criminal, and Czechoslovakia would be seen as an outlaw state in the eyes of the world. No, Gustav Husák conceded, there was

Václav Havel addresses a crowd of more than 200,000 people in Wenceslas Square.

nothing the government could do now but offer to negotiate with the protesters.

The Czechoslovak prime minister, Ladislav Adamec, sent a representative to Civic Forum's headquarters at the Magic Lantern Theater. Adamec was willing to meet with an opposition delegation the next day, the courier said. But the prime minister was adamant that the delegation *not* include Václav Havel. The Communists were not yet ready to meet with a man long portrayed as a chief enemy of the state.

The next morning, Thursday, November 23, a government limousine arrived at the Magic Lantern to transport the Civic Forum delegation to the prime minister's office in Prague Castle. Havel accompanied them to the castle, but was forbidden from entering the prime minister's office. At first the other Civic Forum representatives hesitated; they insisted that Havel, too, must be allowed to take part in the negotiations. But Havel told them to go ahead into the prime minister's office; this was too important an opportunity for the forum to waste. He would remain behind in the lobby and chat with other visitors to the castle. Reluctantly the rest of the Civic Forum representatives agreed to negotiate without Havel. A group calling itself "the bridge" was formed to relay Adamec's comments back to Havel in the lobby, as well as to report Havel's views to those negotiating upstairs.

On Friday, November 24, Alexander Dubček returned to Prague. Accompanied by Havel, he made his way to Wenceslas Square. As Dubček stepped out onto the balcony overlooking the huge throng, there was a gasp from the crowd. Many thought they were seeing a ghost—the specter of a man all but dead for twenty years. There followed just an instant of silence, as people squinted and stared and made sure their eyes were not deceiving them. Then, finally, a thunderous cheer went up. Dubček's face broke into a wide smile. He took off his hat and waved it at the crowd, just as he had done so often in those happy months of the Prague Spring—those days before the tanks came and, with the tanks Husák and his grim years of "normalization."

When Havel stepped out onto the balcony to join Dubček, the roar of the crowd grew even louder. The people cheered wildly as these heroes of two different generations clasped hands. Even though it was a cold, gray November afternoon, the hopes of that spring twenty-one years before were coming to flower again in Prague.

Both Dubček and Havel spoke to the crowd.

Havel (right) hugs former Czech leader Alexander Dubček upon learning that the entire Czech government had resigned.

They then returned to the Magic Lantern, where representatives of the world's news media were eager to ask them questions. The press conference had barely begun when a courier arrived with amazing news: The entire politburo of the Communist Party had just announced its resignation! It was now obvious that the Communists were in complete disarray. On stage, before the eyes of the world, Havel and Dubček embraced warmly. A bottle of champagne was produced and a toast was offered to "a free Czechoslovakia!"[1]

Two days later, on November 26, a second delegation from Civic Forum met with Prime

Opposition leader Havel (left) shakes hands with Czechoslovak Premier Ladislav Adamec at the start of their talks in Prague.

Minister Adamec. This time, the delegation was led by Václav Havel. The prime minister shook the hand of each member of the group, most of whom he remembered from their talks a few days before. However, when he came to Havel, he held out his hand and said, "We don't know each other."

"I'm Havel," came the reply.[2] The prime minister realized that this second round of talks would not be easy for his government.

Adamec agreed that all political prisoners would be released immediately. The government followed through on this promise, and that very evening some of the released prisoners made their way to Prague and the Magic Lantern to take part in Civic Forum's deliberations. But Havel refused to agree to the government's plea to postpone the general strike scheduled for the next day. It would go on as planned.

On the morning of Monday, November 27, Wenceslas Square was crowded again. As the morning wore on and noon grew closer, there was a feeling of excitement in the square, mixed with tension. In most establishments, business seemed to proceed as usual. However, just before noon the atmosphere in the city changed noticeably. Shopkeepers drew the shutters on their windows and hung "Closed" signs on their doors. Factory workers put down their tools, put on their jackets, and walked outside into the cold November air. The Prague subway came to a halt, as did the city bus lines. Taxicab drivers pulled over to the curb. At just one minute before noon, the newscaster on state television announced that he, too, was joining the strike. In full view of the television cameras, he rose from his seat and walked off the set. Replacing him on screen was a group of technicians in Wenceslas Square, announcing that instead of stopping work, they would show their support for the strike by broadcasting it live across the country!

At exactly noon, the general strike began. Prague, usually an active, noisy city of one and a quarter million people, was given over to peace and quiet. The scene was repeated in cities across the land…in Brno…Ostrava…and in Bratislava. From one end of Czechoslovakia to the other, the general strike was an overwhelming success. Millions of Czechs and Slovaks participated, and for two hours the country came to a virtual standstill.

The next day, following a brief meeting with a delegation from Civic Forum, Adamec issued a statement declaring that a new government composed of a "broad coalition" of parties would be formed within five days.

The "broad coalition" offered by the government, however, proved completely unacceptable to the people. Of twenty-one posts in the new government, sixteen would still be held by Communists, many of them well-known supporters of Husák's hard-line policies. Civic Forum wasted no time in rejecting the government's offer.

The mood of the demonstrators in Wenceslas Square became increasingly defiant. When they heard of Adamec's proposals for a "broad coalition," the shout "Resign!" rose from the crowd as though it were speaking in one voice. Other demonstrators sneered at the five positions reserved for non-Communists in the new government and took up the cry "Five crumbs won't feed us!" Others responded, "We are here to stay!"[3]

On the morning of Monday, December 4, a large group of students dressed like Santa Claus (or Saint Nicholas, as he is known in Czechoslovakia) gathered outside the headquarters of the Communist Party. Instead of delivering presents to the party leaders, however, they dumped large bags full of garbage in front of the headquarters. The next morning, another group of students assembled a wall of cardboard boxes 15 feet high in front of the offices of various government ministries. Many government workers on their way to their jobs gave up trying to find a way around the wall and returned home instead.

There were smaller, less public demonstrations as well. In one part of the square, a small group of students held a quiet gathering to commemorate the singer-songwriter John Lennon on the ninth anniversary of his murder. The music of Lennon's song "Imagine" could be heard drifting over the crowds in the center of Prague:

On December 5, 1989, students put up a wall of cardboard boxes at the entrance to government offices to show their disapproval of Czechoslovakia's Communist government.

> *Imagine all the people*
> *sharing all the world . . .*
> *You might say I'm a dreamer,*
> *but I'm not the only one*
> *perhaps some day you'll join us*
> *and the world will live as one. . . .*

Indeed, some of the students' dreams were about to come true. On Thursday, December 7,

Ladislav Adamec resigned as Czechoslovakia's prime minister. He was replaced by a young reform Communist, a man named Márian Calfa. Calfa's first action in office was to invite representatives of Civic Forum and Public Against Violence to reopen negotiations with the government. The opposition accepted Calfa's offer, and a delegation led by Havel left immediately for the castle. After a short negotiating session, an agreement was reached.

Calfa would remain as the country's prime minister until genuinely free elections could be held, sometime in the spring of 1990. A new government would be formed immediately, in which Civic Forum/Public Against Violence would hold seven positions; Communists would hold only ten (of whom two were also members of Civic Forum). The Socialist and People's parties—former allies of the Communists who were now sympathetic to the opposition—would hold two positions each. Two members of Civic Forum/Public Against Violence, Jan Čarnogursky and Valtr Komarek, would serve as vice premiers. Several other important government departments were to be headed by members of the opposition as well.

Perhaps the most intense discussion was over who should now be in charge of the Ministry of the Interior, which included control of the secret police. Finally a compromise was reached on this question: Calfa, Čarnogursky, and Komarek would jointly serve as ministers of the interior. Just days before, Čarnogursky had been on trial in Bratislava, charged with undermining the government. He had been found guilty, of course, and was awaiting sentencing when word arrived that all political prisoners were to be released. He had hurried straight from jail to the Magic Lantern. Now he was to be one of the three men in charge of the state security apparatus!

That evening, Havel read the names of the new government to a jubilant crowd in the square. As each name was read, a great cheer went up from the hundreds of thousands of people gathered below. Jan Čarnogursky . . . Valtr Komarek . . . Jiří Dienstbier . . . Petr Miller . . . men whom the government had held in utter contempt only weeks before. Now these men *were* the government. So much had changed so quickly. At an almost dizzying rate of speed, a revolution had swept Czechoslovakia: a revolution of students and actors and writers and teachers and factory workers and store clerks. A revolution completely without violence. Indeed, the change in Czechoslovakia had been achieved so gently and graceful-

People cheer as they listen to Havel announce the names of Czechoslovakia's first non-Communist dominated government since 1948. Thousands of people gathered in Wenceslas Square to bear witness to the success of their peaceful revolution.

ly that people the world over began to refer to it as the Velvet Revolution.

To many of the revolutionaries in Prague, one goal still remained to be realized. Overnight it seemed, many people began wearing buttons that read "Havel for President." At nearly every mass rally—and especially when Havel himself was in attendance—the cry *"Havel na Hrad!* Havel to the castle!"* filled the air.

On December 10, the cabinet of the new

coalition government was sworn in at Prague Castle by the president of the Socialist Republic of Czechoslovakia, Gustav Husák. For the first time in forty-one years, non-Communists held a majority in the nation's governing council. As soon as the ceremony was finished, Jiří Dienstbier excused himself and went to find a telephone. During the years since his release from prison, he had, of course, been unable to find work in his chosen field as a journalist. Instead, he had supported his family by working as a boiler-room attendant. Now he was foreign minister of his country—but as the oath was being administered, he realized that he had forgotten to arrange for someone to check his boilers that afternoon!

When Husák had finished administering the oaths of office to the new cabinet, he retired to his office deep in one of the castle's many wings. There he put his signature on his letter of resignation. He realized that there would be no place for him in the government of a free Czechoslovakia.

Attention now turned to the selection of a new president. There was little doubt that Václav Havel would be Civic Forum's nominee for the position. At first it appeared as though there might be at least one other nominee. Many reform Communists believed that the presidency should

Czech dissident Václav Havel and his wife, Olga, appear on a balcony overlooking Wenceslas Square on December 11, 1989.

be offered to Alexander Dubček. This, they said, would present a clear symbol to the world that the 1968 Warsaw Pact invasion had been completely repudiated, and that Czechoslovakia intended to proceed quickly down the road of reform. Many others, however, while agreeing that Dubček was an admirable and honest man, nevertheless believed that his time in history was past. The Velvet Revolution no longer sought merely to *reform* the Communist system. The people who gathered in Wenceslas Square in December 1989 would not be satisfied unless that system was completely dismantled.

On December 16, Havel appeared on national television. He told the people of his country that he was willing to become their president. However, he insisted, he would accept the position only if Alexander Dubček was there by his side. Appearing before the press later that evening, Dubček announced his support for Havel, and added, "We have been together from the very start."[4]

That same night, Havel and Dubček attended a reception at the Italian embassy. But instead of joining in the festivities in the embassy's main hall, they met in a small room to work out an agreement. They decided that Havel should become Czechoslovakia's new president. For his part, Dubček would be named chair of the National Assembly.

On December 28 the National Assembly, by a vote of 298 to 0, with one abstention, elected Alexander Dubček as its leader. The next day Prime Minister Calfa appeared before the assembly to place the name of Václav Havel in nomination for the presidency of Czechoslovakia. "He has won the respect of us all," Calfa said. "He never accepted the suggestions of friends or foes that he go into exile, and bore the humiliation of a man oppressed and relegated by those in power to the margins of society." The prime minister concluded, "Your vote for Václav Havel will be a vote for insuring the human rights of every citizen of our country."[5]

The members of the National Assembly then cast their ballots. While there was never any doubt as to the result of the voting, the chamber grew quiet as the clerk prepared to announce the tally. All 323 votes cast in the National Assembly that day supported Václav Havel's candidacy. Havel would be the new president of the Czechoslovak Socialist Republic.

Márian Calfa and Alexander Dubček then left the hall to inform Havel officially of his election.

Two women in folkloric dresses hold a poster of the new Czechoslovakian President, Václav Havel.

A few minutes later, the three men reemerged through the large wooden doors at the back of the old hall. A wave of applause swept the room, growing louder and louder as the trio moved forward toward the podium at the front. Václav Havel had won a great political victory, to be sure. But this day his face did not bear the wide grin that had grown so familiar to his country's people over the past several weeks. Instead, his mood seemed somber and serious, in stark contrast to that of the cheering deputies who surrounded him. Havel sensed the great responsibility being placed on his shoulders, and the great challenges he would face as he made the transition from private citizen to national leader. Gone now was the lighthearted joking and banter with which he had amused the world's press at the Magic Lantern. Gone, too, was the wardrobe he had worn through the weeks of revolution—blue jeans, sport shirts open at the neck, woolen pullover sweaters. Today, for his inauguration, Havel was wearing his only suit. He had had to borrow a necktie, though, for he had not worn one of those in years.

Alexander Dubček administered the oath of office. The words Havel read were almost exactly the same as those Husák had spoken on assuming the presidency in 1975. Havel promised to obey the constitution and laws of the republic, to watch over the interests of the people of the country, and to carry out the duties of his office with fairness and equity. However, unlike Husák, Havel did not have to swear "to defend socialism against all enemies." Just the previous day, the National Assembly had voted to delete that clause from the presidential oath.

Havel walks past an honor guard at Prague Castle after the National Assembly elected him president of Czechoslovakia.

When the swearing-in was completed, Olga Havel joined her husband in the plaza outside Prague Castle. There an army unit fired a twenty-gun salute in honor of the country's new president. The unit then stood at attention as, slowly and deliberately, Havel passed before them in review. The gentle-mannered, intellectual playwright was now the commander in chief of his country's armed forces. What an unlikely role this was f o r Havel, of all people!

That evening the streets of Prague were filled with people joined together in celebration of the victory of the Velvet Revolution. All across the city, people danced in the streets. Some sang patriotic songs just as loudly as they could. That night the sounds of once-forbidden rock and roll shook the windows around Wenceslas Square. Russian champagne flowed freely as numerous toasts were offered. "To Havel! To freedom! To democracy! To Czechoslovakia!" Many people said that the country had never seen such a grand party before. It was even more joyous than the celebrations that had marked the overthrow of Nazi Germany in 1945.

Havel loved a good party as much as anyone. And on this historic evening in Prague, he thoroughly enjoyed watching the crowds as they gathered below his balcony. He would have liked to go downstairs and mingle with them. Perhaps they could even share a toast or two. But it would not be possible; he had no time to linger. The president of Portugal had just arrived for a state visit, and President Václav Havel had to return to Prague Castle to greet him.

Chapter / Ten

A Hard Road Ahead

Václav Havel and other leaders of Civic
Forum/Public Against Violence wasted no time in
assuming their places in the new, democratic government of Czechoslovakia. Within a week,
Finance Minister Václav Klaus was announcing
plans for changes in the country's economy. Soon
the government would begin the process of dismantling the socialist system and the nation
would begin to move down the road to a market
economy. Foreign Minister Jiří Dienstbier traveled
to Břeclav, on the border between Czechoslovakia
and Austria. There, he and Austrian Foreign Minister Alois Mock happily cut away a portion of the

barbed wire fortifications between the two countries. This, they said, symbolized the removal of the iron curtain between Eastern and Western Europe.

In February 1990, less than two months after assuming the presidency, Havel left Czechoslovakia for a trip to the United States. This was his first trip to the West since 1968, when as a young playwright he had traveled to New York City. Now, more than twenty years later, he spent time with some of the friends he had met on that first trip. Together, they revisited many of the places Havel had delighted in during his first visit. In Washington, D.C., Havel met with U.S. President George Bush, and also spoke before a joint session of Congress. In a moving address, the new president of Czechoslovakia recounted for the Congress the amazing story of his country's revolution:

> *The last time they arrested me, on October 27 of last year, . . . I was living in a country ruled by the most conservative Communist government in Europe, and our society slumbered beneath the pall of a totalitarian system. Today, less than four months later, I am speaking to you as the representative of a country that has set out on the road to*

democracy, a country where there is complete freedom of speech, which is getting ready for free elections, and which wants to create a prosperous market economy and its own foreign policy.

Then Havel paused, and in a voice deep with emotion added:

"It is all very strange indeed."[1]

The members of the U.S. Congress leaped to their feet. They realized that the man to whom they were listening was a genuine hero of the twentieth century, a man who had been, throughout his life, a living example of his own philosophy of "living in the truth."

Havel grew increasingly comfortable and confident in his new position as president. Just a short time after he came to office, the Czech tennis star Martina Navratilova presented him with an unusual gift: a shiny red scooter. Havel could make use of it, Navratilova said, when he had to hurry through the castle's labyrinth-like corridors from one important meeting to another. In the happy days following the Velvet Revolution, visitors to Prague would sometimes be treated to the sight of the president of Czechoslovakia racing on his scooter between government offices!

In spite of the increased power Havel's new office gave him, and in spite of the esteem with which he was now viewed by his own people and people the world over, Václav and Olga refused to move into the lavish presidential suite at the castle. Instead, they continued to share an apartment with Václav's brother, Ivan, and his wife on the fourth floor of a building Havel's father had built many years before. There they lived as before, in comfort, though not in elegance. Havel drove himself to work at the castle every morning. When the old elevator in their apartment building broke down, the president of the republic himself would have to lug packages up from the street.

But while Havel was able to make the transition from dissident to president quite smoothly, Czechoslovakia's transition from dictatorship to democracy would prove much more difficult.

The toughest question faced by the country was the matter of Slovakia. Czechs and Slovaks had shared a common area of central Europe for many centuries. However, there had always been deep cultural and social differences between the two peoples. In addition, most Slovaks were devout Catholics, while most Czechs tended toward Protestantism. Historically, there had never been a common state of Czechs and

Slovaks until the Republic of Czechoslovakia was founded in 1918.

After the republic was established, many Slovaks accused the Czechs of trying to dominate them. Some demanded that Slovakia be given the right to govern itself. Nationalist feelings within Slovakia were exploited by the Nazis. A puppet government of an "independent" Slovakia was established following the German invasion of Czechoslovakia in 1939. When the Communists came to power, however, Czechs and Slovaks were reunited into one country, and feelings of Slovak nationalism were held firmly under control. Some of Czechoslovakia's Communist leaders had even been arrogant enough to claim that Communism had "solved the Slovak question." The absurdity of these claims became readily apparent following the 1989 revolution. Increasingly within Slovakia, demands for greater independence from the government in Prague were once again being heard.

Leadership of the nationalist movement in Slovakia soon passed into the hands of Vladimir Meciar. Meciar was a former Communist who had become a member of Public Against Violence at the time of the Velvet Revolution. Following the downfall of the Communist government, Meciar was named prime minister of the government of

Slovakia. However, while Meciar was a staunch nationalist, most of the members of Public Against Violence favored a closer relationship with the central government in Prague. In time, differences of opinion within the Slovak democratic movement turned quite bitter. In April 1991, Havel removed Meciar as prime minister of Slovakia and replaced him with Jan Čarnogursky.

This move angered many nationalists in Slovakia. They declared that it was just one more example of the domination of "Prague intellectuals" over the country's government. Now, when Havel visited Bratislava, he would sometimes be pelted with eggs. His speeches were often interrupted by hecklers demanding that he address them in the Slovak language rather than in his native Czech. Other Slovaks, however, appreciated Havel's efforts to find the proper balance between the Slovak desire for more independence and the interests of the common federation of Czechs and Slovaks.

In June 1992, a second set of free elections was held throughout Czechoslovakia. These illustrated very clearly just how complicated the situation in the country had become. The chief victor in the Czech lands, the Civic Democratic Party led by Václav Klaus, supported Havel in his bid for

Havel with Vladimir Meciar, Slovak Prime Minister and leader
of the Movement for a Democratic Slovakia, at Bratislava
Castle, July 3, 1992

another term as president. However, in Slovakia, the clear winner in the elections was Meciar's Movement for a Democratic Slovakia. This group opposed Havel's reelection and also believed that the federation of Czechs and Slovaks should be dissolved and replaced by a very loose alliance, or even by two separate and independent states. In early July 1992, Meciar and his followers were able to block the National Assembly's reelection of Václav Havel.

It became increasingly apparent that the Czech and Slovak federation was doomed. Unable to negotiate a new alliance, the two parties finally agreed that, on January 1, 1993, Czechoslovakia would split into two separate countries. The Velvet Revolution would be followed by what both sides hoped would be a nonviolent, smooth "velvet divorce."

Havel respected the right of the Slovak people to self-determination. He declared, however, that he would not serve as the "caretaker clerk" presiding over the dismantling of the country.[2] On July 17, the Slovak Parliament in Bratislava approved a declaration of sovereignty, effectively making Slovakia an independent state. Just minutes later, Havel appeared on national television and announced that he would resign from the presidency. The breakup of the country was now inevitable, he said. Later he told representatives of the press, "I prefer to resign before I have to sign something bad."[3] He would not be like his predecessors who had signed the country's death warrant in the days following the Munich conference in 1938. He would not be like those who in 1947 had signed the documents that allowed the Communists to take over the government. No, Havel would leave office rather than condone a course of events he personally opposed.

Czech President Havel waves from a window on his last day in office on July 20, 1992.

Václav Havel would be the last president of a united Czechoslovakia. On January 1, 1993, two new countries came into being: the Czech Republic and the Republic of Slovakia. On January 26, the National Assembly of the Czech Republic elected Václav Havel as its first president.

Havel was very proud to be so honored by his country's people. Yet his own personal advancement had never been the most important consideration in his life.

The most important ideals for Havel, still, were the defense of freedom and the need to live in truth. These had been the underlying themes of all his plays. They had been the reasons behind all his public actions. They had been the principles that had guided him throughout his adult life; the values he had always affirmed, for which he had gone to prison, for which he had risked everything. Now, as one of the most highly respected world leaders, he would not turn his back on freedom and truth.

Freedom. Truth. And hope. The same hope that had guided Václav Havel through the bleak years of Communism remained alive within him, however massive the problems were that needed to be faced along the road into the future. "I cherish a certain hope in me," Havel told the American editor Lance Morrow in 1992, "hope as a state of spirit without which I cannot imagine living or doing something. I can hardly imagine living without hope. As for the future of the world: there is a colorful spectrum of possibilities, from the worst to the best. What will happen, I do not

President Bill Clinton talks with patrons at a pub in downtown Prague in 1994. To his right is Czech President Havel.

know. [But] hope forces me to believe that those better alternatives will prevail, and above all it forces me to do something to make them happen."[4]

The public life of Václav Havel had only begun.

/Chapter Notes

Chapter 1
1. Václav Havel, "Playwright-Dissident Václav Havel Assumes the Presidency of Czechoslovakia," in *Lend Me Your Ears: Great Speeches in History*, ed. by William Safire (New York: W. W. Norton), 629.
2. Ibid., p. 629.

Chapter 2
1. Winston Churchill, "Winston Churchill Warns the West of the Soviet Iron Curtain," in *Lend Me Your Ears*, 791.

Chapter 3
1. Havel, *Disturbing the Peace: A Conversation with Karel Hvížďala* (New York: Alfred A. Knopf, 1990), 40.

Chapter 4
1. Tad Szulc, *Czechoslovakia Since World War II* (New York: Viking Press, 1971), 354.

Chapter 5
1. Havel, *Disturbing the Peace*, 120.
2. Havel, "'Dear Dr. Husák,'" *Open Letters: Selected Writings, 1965—1990* (New York: Vintage Books, 1992), 54.
3. Ibid., 82–83.
4. Havel, *Disturbing the Peace*, xii.

Chapter 6
1. Havel, *Disturbing the Peace*, 128.
2. Edá Kriseová, *Václav Havel: The Authorized Biography* (New York: St. Martin's Press, 1993), 162.

Chapter 7

1. Havel, *Disturbing the Peace*, 151.
2. Ibid., 151.
3. Havel, *Letters to Olga*, 74.
4. Havel, *Disturbing the Peace*, 159.
5. Ibid., 161–162.

Chapter 8

1. Herman Schwartz, "Fueling Demands of Czech Reform," *The Nation*, May 15, 1989, 663.
2. Ibid., 660.

Chapter 9

1. Timothy Garton Ash, *The Magic Lantern: The Revolution of '89 Witnessed in Warsaw, Budapest, Berlin, and Prague* (New York: Random House, 1990), 96.
2. Ibid., 102.
3. *New York Times*, December 5, 1989, 14.
4. *New York Times*, December 17, 1989, 30.
5. *New York Times*, December 30, 1989, 10.

Chapter 10

1. Czechoslovak Embassy to the United States. "Address of the President of the Czechoslovak Republic to a Joint Session of the United States Congress" (Washington, D.C., February 21, 1990).
2. *New York Times*, July 21, 1992, 8.
3. Ibid., 8.
4. Lance Morrow, "'I Cherish a Certain Hope,'" *Time*, August 3, 1992, 48.

Glossary

Allies—France, Great Britain, the Soviet Union, the United States, and the nations that sided with them against the Axis forces during World War II.

bourgeois—The class of people who own property under capitalism. Under Communism, *bourgeois* is a term of reproach aimed at all who oppose the Communist system.

capitalist—Referring to an economic system in which property is owned by private individuals or groups. Under capitalism, the economy is freed from undue government regulation, and free market forces of supply and demand are the determining factors.

coalition—A group composed of members of two or more political parties, joining forces to achieve common objectives.

Communism—An economic and political system in which all property is owned by the state and the society is placed under the control of a single (Communist) party.

conservative—An individual who is slow to embrace political and social change.

dissident—An individual who speaks out in opposition to those in power. The term generally refers to those who oppose their nation's Communist government.

fascist—Referring to a political system characterized by a strong central government. The rights of opposition parties and individuals are severely limited.

liberalism—Belief in the desirability of changes or reforms in a system or institution.

Nazi Party—The fascist political group, headed by Adolf Hitler, that ruled Germany from 1933 to 1945. Its policies included a buildup in the German military; the annihilation of Jews, gypsies, and other groups; and the establishment of German supremacy over all of Europe.

parliamentary democracy—A political system in which voters elect representatives to a legislature (or parliament). The legislators in turn decide who will be the leader of the government.

Appendix Two
Václav Havel: A Time Line

1936   Václav Havel is born in Prague (October 5).

1939–1945   Czechoslovakia is under the domination of Nazi Germany.

1948   The Communist takeover of Czechoslovakia is completed.

1951   Havel goes to work as a laboratory assistant after his high school applications are rejected because of his negative "class profile."

1955   Havel finishes night school classes and receives a high school diploma; he is blocked from attending college by the Communist authorities.

1956   Havel makes an impassioned plea for artistic freedom at a conference for young writers at Dobříš.

1957–1959   Havel serves in the Czechoslovak Army. He helps to form a theater company and writes his first plays.

1959   On his return to Prague, Havel accepts a position as a stagehand at the ABC Theater.

1960–1968   Havel accepts a position as a stagehand and electrician at Prague's

Theater on the Balustrade and eventually rises to the position of dramaturge.

1963 The Theater on the Balustrade presents Havel's first full-length play, *The Garden Party*.

1964 Havel marries Olga Šplíchalová.

1965 Havel's second full-length play, *The Memorandum*, is presented.

1966–1967 Havel is finally allowed to enroll at the Prague Academy of Arts, and he receives his college degree.

1968 Alexander Dubček becomes the leader of Czechoslovakia's Communist Party and institutes a wide-scale program of reform that becomes known as the Prague Spring. However, in August troops from the Soviet Union and other Warsaw Pact nations invade Czechoslovakia. They reinstate hard-line Communist policies, and eventually Dubček is pressured to resign from power.

1970–1972 Havel's name is placed on an official list of writers banned by the Communist authorities, and copies of his works are removed from library shelves around the country.

1974   Havel takes a job in a brewery at Trutnov.

1975   Havel writes to President Husák, blaming him for the depressed state of Czechoslovak society. Later, he starts to publish and distribute the *samizdat* publication *Edice Expedice*; he also completes the plays *Audience* and *Private View*.

1976   Havel helps to found the Czechoslovak human rights group Charter 77.

1977   Havel is subject to continual harassment and detention by the police.

1978   Havel is one of the founders of the Committee for the Defense of the Unjustly Prosecuted (VONS). He is then placed under continual police surveillance, amounting to virtual house arrest. During this time he completes work on "The Power of the Powerless."

1979   Havel is arrested for his work with VONS, and is sentenced to four and a half years in prison.

1980–1983	Havel serves his sentence at the Heřmanice prison camp, near Ostrava, and the prison at Plzeň-Bory.
1983	Because of ill health, Havel is released from prison before completing his term.
1985	Havel reassumes his former position as the chief spokesperson for Charter 77 and VONS.
1989	Havel is arrested in Prague for marking the anniversary of the death of Jan Palach; for this "crime" he is imprisoned for four months. In November massive protests against the Husák government break out in Prague and spread to other cities. Within a few weeks, the nonviolent "Velvet Revolution" topples the Communist regime; on December 29, Václav Havel is elected president of the country.
1990	Havel is reelected to the presidency; however, the Civic Forum movement, which led the revolution, starts to fragment into different political parties.

1992	Vladimir Meciar's Movement for a Democratic Slovakia becomes a dominant political force in the eastern part of the country and begins advocating full independence from Prague. Meciar's supporters block Havel's reelection to the presidency. Following the Slovak assembly's declaration of sovereignty, Havel resigns from office.
1993	The Czech Republic is formed as a result of the breakup of Czechoslovakia, and Havel is elected as its first president.

Selected Bibliography

Ash, Timothy Garton. *The Magic Lantern: The Revolution of '89 Witnessed in Warsaw, Budapest, Berlin, and Prague.* New York: Random House, 1990.

Frankland, Mark. *The Patriots' Revolution: How Eastern Europe Toppled Communism and Won Its Freedom.* Chicago: Ivan R. Dee, 1992.

Havel, Václav. *Disturbing the Peace: A Conversation with Karel Hvížďala.* New York: Alfred A. Knopf, 1990.

Havel, Václav. *The Garden Party and Other Plays.* New York: Grove Press, 1993.

Havel, Václav. *Largo Desolato.* New York: Grove Weidenfeld, 1985.

Havel, Václav. *Letters to Olga: June 1979–September 1982.* New York: Henry Holt, 1989.

Havel, Václav. *Living in Truth: Twenty-two Essays Published on the Occasion of the Awarding of the Erasmus Prize to Václav Havel.* London: Faber and Faber, 1986.

Havel, Václav. *The Memorandum.* New York: Grove Weidenfeld, 1967.

Havel, Václav. *Open Letters: Selected Writings, 1965–1990.* New York: Vintage Books, 1992.

Havel, Václav. *Temptation*. New York: Grove Weidenfeld, 1986.

Kriseová, Edá. *Václav Havel: The Authorized Biography*. New York: St. Martin's Press, 1993.

Kusin, Vladimir V. *From Dub∑ek to Charter 77: A Study of the "Normalization" in Czechoslovakia*. New York: St. Martin's Press, 1978.

Moritz, Charles, ed. *Current Biography Yearbook, 1985*. New York: H. W. Wilson, 1985.

Rakowska-Harmstone, Teresa, and Andrew Gyorgy, eds. *Communism in Eastern Europe*. Bloomington: Indiana University Press, 1979.

Shirer, William L. *The Rise and Fall of the Third Reich: A History of Nazi Germany*. New York: Simon & Schuster, 1960.

Starr, Richard F. *The Communist Regimes in Eastern Europe*. Stanford, Calif.: Hoover Institution on War, Revolution and Peace, 1971.

Szulc, Tad. *Czechoslovakia Since World War II*. New York: Viking Press, 1971.

Szulc, Tad. *The Invasion of Czechoslovakia, August, 1968: The End of a Socialist Experiment in Freedom*. New York: Franklin Watts, 1974.

Index

DATE DUE